HUMANS AND THEIR ENVIRONMENT
BEYOND THE NATURE/CULTURE OPPOSITION

ENVIRONMENTAL HUMANITIES SERIES: 1

Humans and Their Environment, Beyond the Nature/Culture Opposition

By Claude Calame

First published in 2023 by Transnational Press London in the United Kingdom, 13 Stamford Place, Sale, M33 3BT, UK.
www.tplondon.com

Transnational Press London® and the logo and its affiliated brands are registered trademarks.

Requests for permission to reproduce material from this work should be sent to: sales@tplondon.com

Paperback
ISBN: 978-1-80135-184-3
Digital
ISBN: 978-1-80135-185-0

Cover Design: Nihal Yazgan
Cover image by Joshua Earle on unsplash.com

Transnational Press London Ltd. is a company registered in England and Wales No. 8771684.

HUMANS
AND THEIR
ENVIRONMENT
BEYOND THE
NATURE/CULTURE OPPOSITION

Claude Calame

TRANSNATIONAL PRESS LONDON

2023

CONTENTS

PREFACE TO THE ENGLISH EDITION

Repeated heat waves, persistent droughts, devastating fires: the summer of 2022 has proved to be "Europe's hottest on record". This is the finding of a report from Copernicus, the European Union's Earth observation programme. Never before had the temperature exceeded 40°C in the rainy UK. Compared with average summer temperatures in Europe, over the period 1999-2020 (which were already high) the average for this summer was 1.34°C higher. And this is nothing compared to the rains and floods that have devastated both Pakistan and Nigeria. In Pakistan, flooding caused almost 2,000 deaths, leaving 33 million people effectively homeless; in Nigeria, there were more than 600 deaths and 1.3 million people displaced. Once again it is the poorest countries that are bearing the brunt of the ecological consequences of the lifestyles of the richest countries and those who dominate them.

Despite these unmistakable and worrying developments, the latest report by the IPCC (Intergovernmental Panel on Climate Change) had to sound the alarm once again on the lack of concerted global action. To achieve the objectives set in 2015 in Paris at COP21, promoted by the United Nations Framework Convention on Climate Change – notably, to limit the increase in average global temperatures to 1.5°C by the end of the century – global greenhouse gas emissions must be reduced by 43% by 2030. Yet, after a pause due to the restrictions caused by the Covid-19 pandemic, global emissions of these gases reached a new record in 2021.

The results of COP26 in Glasgow last November, at the end of a summer that was just as worrying climatically as the one we have just experienced, raised serious doubts. Given the feeble commitments made by states – non-binding measures that amount to little more than greenwashing – we can expect a projected global temperature increase of 2.4°C. At the time of writing, the decisions just taken at COP27, at Sharm El Sheikh in Egypt, are hardly more encouraging, with the exception that an agreement has finally been reached to establish a "loss and damage" fund to address climate impact in developing countries whose contribution to the climate crisis bears no comparison to our own. Even so, it remains unclear where these funds are going to come from…

As for the causes of global warming, the preamble of the IPCC report is clear: 'It is unequivocal that human influence has warmed the atmosphere, ocean and land. Widespread and rapid changes in the atmosphere, ocean, cryosphere and biosphere have occurred'. It is therefore more pressing than ever to address the foundations of humans' relationship with their environment, particularly with regard to our inveterate use of techniques and technologies with the sole aim of pursuing economic growth and the financial profits to be made of it.

Admittedly, the IPCC report made several proposals to break the deadlock and meet the unambitious targets of the 2015 Paris Agreement: the production of less carbon-intensive energy, the reduction of energy demands in food, housing, work, and transport, and the development of more compact, pedestrian-friendly cities. Yet it did not even begin to question the very system underpinning the destructive deterioration of the relationship between human communities and their environment: globalised capitalism, based on a form of growth that obeys purely economic and financial imperatives. The logics of profit and the market reduce the environment to a store of 'natural resources', while also reducing the work of men and women to a store of 'human resources'…

In fact, what is at issue is the objectification of the environment as a 'nature' whose resources can be exploited by human labour according to a purely economic and financial logic, for the sake of so-called human progress measured obsessively in terms of 'growth' and increased GDP.

As both a Hellenist-citizen and a mountaineer shocked by the melting of Alpine glaciers, I could not remain indifferent to a series of forms of pollution that threaten the very future of humanity in its various social and cultural communities. Indeed, the matter at hand is the relationship of humans, in their various practices, with the environment, which, moreover, ensures their survival. I was therefore led to examine from a distance, as an anthropologist, some of the conceptions that the Greek *sophoí* had of the relations of mortal humans with their milieu, in particular by means of the idea of *phúsis*, which cannot be reduced to the modern concept of 'nature'. This exercise is not aimed at finding in ancient Greece a model for us to follow now, but rather at allowing us to bring a new critical perspective to bear on the contemporary 'cultural' paradigm.

After the original publication in French of this essay in historical and critical anthropology, and a subsequent edition in an Italian translation, the publication of this new edition in English can be seen as the third stage of a comparative itinerary that I originally undertook in 2015, on the eve of COP21 in Paris.

After the first edition, my work on this subject was nourished by several events and exchanges: to begin with, two debates at the École des Hautes Études en Sciences Sociales in Paris, one of which took place in the context of the seminar led by Augustin Berque. The essay also benefited from discussions of the text in meetings of the 'Hésiode' research group (Histoire et Épistémologie des Savoirs et des Idées aux Origines De l'Écologie), on the initiative of Amarande Laffon (University of Nantes) and William Pillot (University of Angers). Later, within the framework of the Associazione Italiana di Cultura Classica 'Antico e moderno', several discussions were organised with classes from different Licei classici in Italy. These exchanges led to the Italian edition of the essay, in Franco Giorgianni's translation, which was published by the Palermo publisher Sellerio in 2021, on the eve of the COP26 in Glasgow.

This Italian edition was complemented and enriched by the publication of two studies, by Andrea Cozzo (2021) and Franco Giorgianni (2021) respectively.

The former focused on the sensitivity of Greek sages and philosophers to the climatic disasters that their ancestors may have faced, leading to large movements of people which we would now term as 'environmental migration'. Cozzo's study also highlights certain strategic interventions on the environment and the territory for the sake of power, such as Xerxes's attempt to subjugate the Hellespont by chaining it like a slave and thus trying to change its 'rhythm'. In so doing, Xerxes interfered with that which had been established by *phúsis*, but by bridging the strait and piercing Mount Athos he also disrupted, according to Herodotus's account, both the work of the gods and the intentions of men. Another form of interference in the environment is the exploitation of the earth's precious metals through mining, often driven by the desire to accumulate wealth. The role of the philosophers in this case was to raise awareness of the limits that must not be exceeded, and to encourage moderation, both in terms of living the 'good life' and in the pursuit of political balance.

Giorgianni's study considers the uses that are made of the technical arts, the *tékhnai*, whose invention is attributed to Prometheus. This leads him to address two fundamental questions: first, that of the impact on the environment of the means that we use to interact with it, and second, that of the criteria that govern these uses. Two important perspectives, which I address further in the present edition, are brought to bear in the Hippocratic reflection on the influence of the climate on the morphology and character of humans: firstly, an essential element is the interpretation of the observed relations between the climatic conditions due to the seasons, the character of the territories concerned, and the 'nature' of the humans who inhabit them; secondly, in the relationship between *phúsis* and *nómos*, the technical arts are indispensable for allowing humans to construct themselves, socially and culturally, in an interactive and balanced relationship with a particular ecosystem.

The work of these two authors has allowed me, for this third edition, now in English, to deepen my critical and politically engaged analysis of the interaction between human communities and their environment, and of the challenges posed by our current inveterate use of techniques and technologies according to a purely economic, financial, and consumerist logic. This revised third edition of the essay on the humans and their environment has been inluenced by my exchanges particularely around the article of 2020-21 first with Salvatore Engel-Di Mauro, editor in chief of Capitalsm Nature Socialism (at SUNY New Paltz), then with Pauline LeVen, at Yale University, and finally on the occasion of a seminar organized by Marianne Hopman and her colleagues at Northwestern University. On the other hand as a reprsentative of the group "Ensemble à gauche" at the city council of Lausanne during the last years I had the opportunity to discuss, along the lines presented here, about the "climate plan" now adopted by the town. The collaboration with Johann Dupuis on that matter has been a source of practical inspiration.

I would also like to express my sincere gratitude to the translator of the present edition of this essay, Sam Ferguson. His attention to the peculiarities of the French language and his sensitivity to the problems posed in the essay have led him to ask questions that have frequently allowed me to clarify, if not correct, my remarks. I am similarly grateful to my colleagues Peggy Karpouzou and Nikoleta Zampaki for hosting this essay in the Environmental Humanities Book Series of Transnational Press London.

Finally, as a prelude, let us reread the choral song that marks the beginning of Sophocles's *Antigone* (verses 332-383). The chorus, made up of the elders of Thebes, sings of the technical arts that allow humans to survive despite their fragile mortal condition: they mention navigation, by which humans cross the sea carried by the wind, hunting and fishing to catch birds and fish, and agriculture with the use of the plough, which allows humans to work the Earth, 'the most powerful of the goddesses, the indestructible, the tireless'. Such practices as the domestication of beasts of burden with the yoke, the construction of shelters, or the concoction of medicines to escape diseases are all examples of the use of 'ingenious means' (*mekhanaí*, verse 349). Ingenious means conceived, as we will see, not as mechanical means as Francis Bacon will later do, but as semiotic, interpretive means. The chorus concludes by singing: 'Holder of industrious knowledge of technical art (*tékhne*, verse 365), man sometimes takes the path of evil, sometimes that of good'.

Thus, in relation to an environment that, from Descartes onwards, we have objectified as a set of 'natural' resources to be exploited by our technical means, the exercise of this practical knowledge evoked by Sophocles's chorus has a twofold outcome: it can lead to good if the laws of the land and the justice of the gods are respected, but it leads to evil if arrogance prevails. The warning is clear. Man can go from being *húpsipolis* to *ápolis*: from occupying a foremost position in the city, to being excluded from it. However the practice of our technical arts is accomplished, it takes place in the social context of the civic community, with consequences both for the practical and cultural orientation of that society and for the environment with which it interacts.

Claude Calame, November 2022

INTRODUCTION

The modern concept of "nature" was forged in Europe from the seventeenth century onwards. A long-standing and tenacious Eurocentric tradition holds that the idea of "nature" as an objective entity can be traced back to the ancient Greek concept of *phúsis*. But what, exactly, is the truth of the matter? This is a question of strategic importance at a time when, among other environmental problems, the climate emergency is causing ever-growing concern about the impact of human activities, and consequently of "culture", upon this nature-object.

When we speak of ancient Greek culture, we are speaking of a culture that is distant from our own in both time and space. This social and cultural difference undoubtedly calls for an anthropological approach. However, a (historical) anthropology of the manifestations of ancient Greek culture requires not only a return to the categories and concepts of the culture in question, with their own indigenous representations and definitions, but also – precisely because of our constant historical contacts with ancient, and especially Classical Greece – a reflexive examination of our own concepts.

This work of critical anthropology, with its potential to open up an indirect perspective on ourselves, is not undertaken here purely for the sake of a genealogical and scholarly analysis of the history of the modern structural opposition between "nature" and "culture"; it is also intended to demonstrate the critical implications of the anthropological approach with regard to the paradigm that underpins our own society, with all its practical consequences. This is none other than the paradigm imposed by neoliberal capitalism, that dogma that, very briefly speaking, has come to dominate and shape – economically, financially, and ideologically – the world of humans and their communities, in their productions and in their relations with one another.

The goal of this short essay is therefore to draw upon an

anthropological understanding of concepts from Greek antiquity, with all the scholarly work that this entails, in order to examine, in a mode of political critique, not only the ideological and practical causes, but also the social and especially environmental consequences, of contemporary changes in the biosphere (notably, but not exclusively related to climate change).

The Greek concept of *phúsis*, which seems to correspond to the modern concept of "nature", refers to the dynamic process by which an organism develops, together with the result of that process. This concept therefore invites us to consider, from this point of view, the technical and interpretative arts that Prometheus offers to mortals, as depicted in Aeschylus's play *Prometheus Bound*; these arts underpin, both intellectually and practically, the signifying relations of humans with their environment. This double reference to Classical Greece will allow us to reflexively re-examine the modern concept of "nature", while also drawing on the perspectives provided by two fields of knowledge based on cutting-edge technologies: genetics and neural sciences respectively. The epistemological principles underlying these two fields of knowledge, which are based on plasticity and interaction, make it possible to revisit the opposition between culture and nature, which then no longer appears as an opposition between the culture of humans and a nature-object, but rather as a dense network of complex and interactive relations between humans and their milieu. When the environment is thus understood as a biosphere, it no longer constitutes an objective and mechanical nature that can be dominated by humans, but rather an element that is simultaneously configured by humans and also indispensable to them.

Once the environment is understood in this way, as the indispensable milieu of humans' practices and interrelations, it cannot be reduced to a concept of nature as a stock of "resources" to be consumed by humans for the sake of individual profit – mainly in the sense of material and financial profit. Such a move therefore undermines the principles of productivism and profit that are the foundation of the capitalist economy. Neither humans nor their environment can be viewed as resources to be exploited without incurring destructive consequences for both the milieu and the most deprived populations. We are then far removed from a vision of, on the one hand, a nature that is passively subjected to human reason and, on the other hand, a human culture capable, by means of its technical arts, of taking advantage of this nature and its forces.

On this basis, I am led to propose once again the anthropological concept of "anthropo-poiesis"; it includes the various and complex processes of the physical and psychic construction of human beings through their social, political, cultural, and even religious interactions with others. However, it is now also necessary to grasp and take into account the impact of the anthropopoietic relations of humans with an environment which is indispensable to their development: the idea of the social and cultural constructedness of human communities must take into account ecologies shaped by the semiotic and technical practices of humans. Both the climate emergency and the finite character of resources that have nothing "natural" about them call for a transition to an altermondialist ecosocialism. This transition requires a break with a capitalism that destroys people and environments, and the reestablishment of interaction between human societies and their milieux in an anthropopoietic and eco-poietic spirit of collaborative construction of human beings. The survival of both humans and their milieux is at stake. In short, "anthropopoiesis" is also "ecopoiesis", and nature can only ever be culture.

The sequence of reflection outlined above is the basis for the five chapters of this short essay. The first chapter is devoted to ancient Greece, with an exploration of the concepts of *phúsis* and *nómos* – the counterparts of the modern concepts of nature and culture – as well as that of *tékhnē*, or technical art. Next, still from the perspective of historical anthropology, I address some of the stages of the modern construction of the concept of culture in relation to a nature-object. The third chapter is devoted to two contemporary fields of biotechnological knowledge, genetics and neural sciences, which invite us to rethink the relations between humans and their environment in terms of porosity and plasticity. In the next chapter, these interactive relations allow a comparison, from a decentred perspective, with the Greek conceptions of *phúsis*. Finally, that critical encounter will allow us to set out the need for an altermondialist transition towards an ecosocialism inspired by the principles of anthropopoiesis and ecopoiesis.

*

The five parts of this essay have benefited from the careful reading and useful suggestions of Philippe Corcuff and Mondher Kilani. I am sincerely grateful to them both. In addition to an interview with Robert Lochhead, whom I thank for his ongoing attention, some of the ideas developed here were discussed in two seminars at the École des Hautes Etudes en Sciences Sociales (EHESS): the one led by Augustin Berque and Luciano Boi on "Mésologies", and one that I co-organise together with Sandra Boehringer, Carole Boidin, Florence Dupont, and Pierre Vesperini, entitled "Prendre les anciens au mot" ("Taking the ancients at their word"). On the occasion of one of these seminars, the comparative reflections presented here were the subject of a very stimulating exchange with Alessandro Buccheri, who devoted his doctorate, based at the University of Siena and the EHESS, to Greek botanical images of the human, with reference to the concept of *phúsis*. These reflections were also presented in two successive lectures at the University of Palermo, at the invitation of Franco Giorgianni, in the framework of the project for a historical lexicon of genetics. Finally, some parts of the ideas presented here were published for the first time in the online journal of ATTAC, *Les Possibles*, issue 3, 2014; thanks are due to Jean-Marie Harribey and Pierre Khalfa for their critical reading of those texts. And it is thanks to Michel Surya's unwavering and benevolent efforts that this essay has been first published in French by the publisher "Lignes", that he is the chief editor of.

Having spent a summer divided between my computer keyboard and

Alpine paths, I hope that I will not embarrass either Philippe Gay or Jean-Claude Pont by dedicating this short militant essay to them. The former, a geologist and mountain guide, led me to the summit of three of the beautiful rocky ridges of the Valais Alps, between Arolla and Zermatt, with a firm grip on the rope that, like the thread of the Fates, guaranteed my safety. The latter, as a professor of the history of sciences as a former professor of the history of sciences at the University of Geneva and founder of the Sierre-Zinal race, provided me with the opportunity to cover once again, at the tempo of a joint Alpine trail, one of the most aesthetic itineraries across the extraordinary high sided valleys leading to the Rhône.

Although I do not ask them to share the positions set out here, either environmentally or politically, I would like to express to both of them the surprising affinities that I feel between, on the one hand, the practical development, in the course of writing, of a long argument in which the guiding line determines the various resistances and turnings, and, on the other hand, the course of a climb or brisk walk, with its rhythmic tension and its physical adherence to the irregularities of an uneven terrain: in both cases I experienced vital and practical rhythms, marked by the intention of anthropo-poietic accomplishment with others, and also marked by the dynamic movement of opera arias, from the "canzonetta sull'aria" in Mozart's *Marriage of Figaro* to the aria of the forging of the sword Notung in Wagner's *Siegfried*. But I shall leave all that for another essay.

On the eve of COP21 in Paris for the publication of the original essay in 2015, and now on the eve of COP27 in Sharm el-Sheikh, I hope that the arguments set out here will be as convincing (if not as aesthetically pleasing), in their discursive development, as the Alpine routes that inspired them. In any case, these mountain journeys have helped to convince me of the complex interactions between our human practices, with their cultural dimension, and the indispensable physical and social environment that allows them to be deployed.

BETWEEN NATURE AND CULTURE

The binary and contrasting distinction between nature and culture was, in a way, canonised by the structuralist thought that reached its peak in the 1970s. In the Francophone context, it has two main sources.

On the one hand, there is the well-known conclusion that René Descartes draws from physics, as a field of knowledge that is "useful for life", in the *Discourse on Method* (published in Leiden in 1637). Physics, as the field of knowledge concerned with "the force and the actions of fire, water, air, the stars, the heavens, and all the other bodies that surround us", is capable, when directed towards appropriate uses, of making us "masters and possessors of nature".[1] Through this understanding of physics, our environment is then not only objectified as a physical nature, but it is also a nature that can be dominated by man, with a utilitarian perspective; in this particular case, the aim is to provide for humans' food and health.

The other main source is to be found among the representatives of the Enlightenment, whose universalising reflection on human societies had two major implications for the conception of nature and culture.

On the one hand, they posited an objectified "nature" in opposition to the faculty of reason, which they considered to be possessed exclusively by human beings. This faculty of reason is defined in terms of its autonomy, having been newly freed from the power of divine origin and supernatural authorities. Nature thus becomes a nature-object on which man, as a reasonable being, can act, exploiting its resources. According to one of the definitions proposed by d'Alembert in the *Encyclopédie*, nature is "the order and natural course of things, the sequence of second causes, or the laws of motion that God has established".[2] Nature corresponds here to

---

[1] Descartes, 1637/1998: 35.

[2] D'Alembert, 1765: 40. To be added would be of course the determinig contribution of Francis Bacon

physical nature, subject to the laws formulated by Newton, but still created by God.

On the other hand, the opposition between nature and human culture became instrumental in guiding an anthropological vision of the development of the human being, in both its phylogenesis and its ontogenesis: the development from nature to culture is here conceived as a development from the animal to the human, conceived as a transition both from the primitive to the civilised and from the imperfection of childhood to the maturity of adulthood. In this anthropological perspective, situated between anthropology as the physical science of man and anthropology as knowledge about human societies and cultures, nature corresponds less to man's material and worldly environment than to the animal and biological dimension of the human species in general.

The distinction thus drawn between nature and culture was subsequently integrated into the semantics of binary oppositions inspired by structuralism. This approach established a separation between two orders that, in reality, prove to be largely permeable with one another. Structuralist anthropologists, while being the architects of that often naturalised opposition between nature and culture, were also the first to relativise its scope:

> *The discontinuity between the two rules [nature and culture] is undoubtedly universally recognized, and there is no society – be it ever so humble – which does not place high value on the arts of civilization, through the discovery and usage of which man differs from animals. Among the peoples called "primitive", however, the notion of nature always offers an ambiguous character. Nature is preculture and it is also sub-culture. But it is by and large the means [as "supernature"] through which man may hope to enter into contact with ancestors, spirits, and gods.[3]*

as far as the mechanical uses of and the dominion for society over a feminine nature are concerned: see, in an ecofeminist perspective, the foundational pages by Merchant 1980: 164-191.

Except where indicated otherwise, translation from languages other than English are our own.

[3] Lévi-Strauss, 1973/1978: 320.

It is against this background that I am undertaking the short semantic journey presented here, using a politically engaged approach of historical and critical anthropology. My starting point will be nature as it was conceived in relation to human culture in ancient Greek thought, to be considered in a logic of "difference" compared to our own cultural paradigm.[4] As indicated in the introduction, this anthropological encounter with the Greek concept of *phúsis*, with its various meanings, will allow us to adopt an indirect and critical perspective on the modern opposition canonised by structuralism. Indeed, taking an anthropological approach to the manifestations of Greco-Roman culture involves not only devoting attention to the categories embedded in that culture, with their own indigenous definitions and contexts, but also undertaking a critical re-examination of our own concepts, if only because of the indirect gaze produced by any anthropological approach.

In the present case, a reflection on the climatic and environmental consequences of the actions of humans and of their cultural practices in relation to an environment objectified as nature, leads us to adopt an attitude of political criticism. What are the implicit uses of the concepts of "nature" and "culture" in our current economic and ideological paradigm, which governs our social organisation and practices, particularly in their relations with the milieu and, more broadly, the biosphere on which our very survival depends?

Through the naturalisation of the "cultural" rules of the market, the milieu is reduced to a nature conceived as a stock of resources ready to be exploited, just as the labour power of workers, conceived as "human resources", is exploited for financial gain. Meanwhile, culture is reduced to the action of individuals in competition with one another, and essentially driven by the profit motive, with

---

[4] Greco-Roman antiquity was presented as a "territory of gaps" by Dupont, 2013: 279-301, following a research seminar entitled "Antiquité au present" ("Antiquity in the Present"), co-organised between the Université de Paris Diderot – Paris 7 (Institut des humanités; Centre Parisien d'Études Critiques) and the EHESS (the AnHiMA research centre). Accordingly, from 2013 this seminar came to be devoted to "Antiquité, territoires des écarts" ("Antiquity, Territories of Gaps"), and was held for several years at the EHESS (CRAL and AnHiMA research centres) under the title "Prendre les Anciens au mot: ce que l'Antiquité fait à la modernité" ("Taking the Ancients at their word: what Antiquity does to modernity").

destructive consequences – as has now been widely recognised – on an environment and human communities that are in constant interaction. Indeed, when, with the help of certain ancient Greek thinkers, we reconceive nature as a milieu, it becomes evident that it is shaped by the various ways of life of humans, with the different technical arts that constitute them and make life possible – in an interaction that was illustrated on the Athenian stage by Aeschylus's *Prometheus Bound*. Similarly, the model of plasticity and permeability, now emerging from both neuroscience and the life sciences, indicates that humans cannot create themselves physically and culturally without interacting with a milieu that they modify in turn through their technical and cultural practices.

This short reflection should demonstrate the need for the ecosocialist stance mentioned above, one that breaks from the (now capitalist) domination of humans over a nature reduced to set of resources, to be replaced by human communities' democratic oversight and use of their animal, vegetal, and physical environment. Furthermore, such an ecosocialist stance calls for an ecopoietics that rejects the Anglo-American neoliberal model of exploitation of natural and human resources for the sake of economic and financial profit; instead it values the anthropopoietic potential of a milieu that is implicated, inextricably and indispensably, in the cultural shaping of the human being in society.

I

HUMANS AND THEIR MILIEU IN ANCIENT GREECE

Let us first point out that in Classical Greece, the term *phúsis*, notwithstanding any controversies and misunderstandings over its meaning, referred to the idea of the formation and development of an entity, a being – whether that being belongs to the animal, vegetal, or physical domain. Two ideas that are fundamental to this conception are that of "accomplishment as becoming" and that of "process as objective realisation". In terms of etymology and morphology, the word clearly derives from the verb *phúein/phúesthai*, meaning "to generate", "to be born", "to grow", and "to become"; as such, its uses are often contextually related to the verb *gígnesthai*, meaning "to become", from the root *gen-*, which also happens to be found in the name of the modern field of genetics! In metaphorical uses of the term, the reference is generally to the growth of a plant. Via the verb *phúein*, *phúsis* therefore implies both a processual and a resultative aspect: accordingly, we find in the *Iliad* certain verses playing etymologically on the *phúllon* (leaf) and *genéē* (generation) in order to compare the successive generations of humans with the blossoming of the leaves of trees each spring and their fall in autumn:

> *Even as are the generations of leaves* [phúllon genéē]*, such are those also of men.*
>
> *As for the leaves* [phúlla]*, the wind scattereth some upon the earth, but the forest,*
>
> *as it bourgeons, putteth forth* [phúei] *others when the season of spring is come;*
>
> *Even so of men one generation* [genée] *springeth up and another passeth away.*[1]

---

[1] Homer, *Iliad* 6, 146-149. English translation from Homer, 1924. See the semantic analysis of the term *phúsis* proposed by Benveniste, 1975: 78-85, together with the necessary clarifications provided by Buccheri, 2012: 141-147, and to be published. Macé, 2012: 54-62, clearly notes that its meaning is grounded in plant growth.

1. The *Phúsis* of the Greek Physiologists

Whatever their etymology, it was in terms of *phúein* and *phúsis* that the so-called "pre-Socratic philosophers" attempted to describe the various processes of generation and development of the world and its component parts.[2] In principle, the perspective adopted by these philosophers, whom we could more accurately call the pre-Platonic "physicists" or "physiologists", was directed towards the search for material causes, while avoiding recourse to any divine force in the description of the processes driving the development of external reality. However, the thought of the Greek physiologists ranged from the emergence of the cosmos to the processes of human development, and by means of metaphor they established a series of relationships between the process of vegetal growth and the process of the engendering of human beings. *Phúsis* was one such metaphor:

> *I will tell you something else. For none of the mortal beings*
>
> *is there birth* [phúsis]*, or an end to destructive death,*
>
> *but only a mixture and exchange* [diállaxis] *of mixed elements;*
>
> *it is men who call this "nature"* [phúsis]*.[3]*

These words were composed by Empedocles in epic verse with its dactylic rhythm; they are found in the first book of a didactic poem later called the *Phusiká*. Birth and death, and consequently *phúsis* in a sense that seems to correspond to our modern concept of "nature", are only the way that a physical process of change, taking place through successive associations and dissociations, appears to humans' eyes. But we should not forget these famous verses of the same Empedocles:

> *Double is my speech. Indeed, sometimes a single being grows out of several,*
>
> *sometimes it divides* [diéphu] *becoming the plural of the one that it was.*

---

[2] See Lloyd, 1991: 91-107.

[3] Fr. 31 B 8 Diels-Kranz (= 22. Emp. D52 Laks-Most). On the controversial question of the number of Empédocles's poems and their respective titles, see Trépanier, 2004: 1-30.

Double is the growth (génesis) of mortal things,

double is their disappearance [...].

Sometimes, by the effect of Love, they all converge into one,

sometimes each is carried separately, as a result of Strife's hatred.[4]

The physical process of growth and dispersion, which extends to all beings, is thus driven by two apparently deified forces: *Philotès* and *Néikos*, Love (which unites beings through reciprocity) and Strife (which separates beings through rivalry).

Let us recall that, in the more abstract perspective developed later, Aristotle postulated that all beings that exist "by nature" have in themselves a principle of movement and stability; this is in contrast to crafted objects such as a bed or an item of clothing, which are products of a technical art (*tékhnē*) and do not possess, implanted (*émphuton*) in their *phúsis*, any impulse to change. Thus all things that exist, all things that have an essence, have within them a "nature"; and this *phúsis* corresponds to a principle of movement that is both form (*morphḗ*) and figure (*eîdos*). The result is a being "by nature" (*phúsei*), in act rather than in power, such as the human. Form is nature, and from a human a human is born.[5]

Furthermore, the doctor of the Hippocratic school who devoted a famous treatise to the "sacred disease" of epilepsy states from the outset that there is nothing more divine or sacred about this disease than other diseases. Just as all other illnesses have an origin (*phúsis*) from which they derive, the "sacred disease" itself has a "nature" (*phúsis*) and a "cause" (*próphasis*).[6] This means, presumably, that all disease is driven by a principle of internal development and growth, which is itself triggered by an external cause.

The dynamic process of development implied by the concept of *phúsis* was thus transferred from the cosmos and the vegetal world to

---

[4] Fr. 31 B 17, 1-3 and 7-8 (= 22. Emp. D73, 1-3 and 7-8 Laks-Most).

[5] Aristotle, *Physics* II, 192b 8-37 and 193a 28-b 12; for Plato (*Laws* 891c and 892c), the principle that drives all things that pertain to *phúsis* (including fire, water, earth, and air) is the soul (*psukhḗ*).

[6] Hippocrates, *On the Sacred Disease* 1, 1.

the human. Yet the idea of a dynamic nature of the human being is constitutive of an anthropology, in the sense of a conception of the human race. The Greeks, implicitly or explicitly, questioned what it is that makes a human a human – and notably a human being that is marked by mortality, since this is what, in the polytheistic regime of the Greek city states, distinguished the human being from the divine.

2. Greek Definitions of the Human and Culture

In ancient Greece, human beings – *ánthrōpos* in the singular, or *ánthrōpoi* in the plural – were viewed as belonging to a category of their own; and this was the case at least as early as the composition of Homeric poetry, in which the human race is defined precisely by its mortality, in contrast to the immortality of the gods. As an example, consider, in the *Iliad*, the words with which Apollo holds back Diomedes in his attempts to slay Aeneas: "Take heed, son of Tydaeus, and turn back! Do not harbour thoughts equal to those of the gods! The race [*phûlon*] of the immortal gods and the race of men who walk the earth will never be equal".[7] The term "race", or rather "kind", is used here because etymologically there is a difference between immortals and mortals that lies in the order of *phúein*: both have their own processes of vital development. Moreover, the *ánthrōpoi* – a category that includes men (*ándres*) and women (*gunaîkes*) – are also called, from Homeric poetry onwards, *brotoí*, which is a word formed from the same root as the Latin *mortuus*: they are mortals, who, as such, are distinguished from the immortals, or *ámbrotoi*.[8]

As for the *Odyssey*, it is generally speaking in contrast to the divine that Odysseus tries to identify the different beings, whether male or female, whom he encounters during his wanderings in the western Mediterranean. This geographical space does not really correspond to the Greece of the Homeric world, and is rather mapped onto an anthropology of myth and fiction. On his floating island, Aeolus,

---

[7] Homer, *Iliad* 5, 440-42.

[8] For example, *Iliad* 22, 8-9, and *Odyssey* 1, 31-32.

dear to the immortals, lives like a god, whereas the scout that Odysseus sends out on his first encounter with Circe wonders whether she is a goddess or a mortal; as it turns out, her powers of erotic seduction and magical cunning place the beautiful woman on the side of the divine.[9]

But the definition of humanity sketched out by Odysseus's narration of his return from Troy uses another point of comparison, situated at the other end of the spectrum from the divine: not the animal world, but rather the world of monsters. The mighty Laestrygonians are more like Giants than men (here *ándres* and not *ánthropoi*).[10] The Cyclopes are also related to the Giants. These monstrous beings have various characteristics that set them apart from humans: from the outset, they are presented as violent, recognising neither laws nor gods; they live in isolation from one another, lacking any kind of assemblies or social and political life; there are no religious practices among the Cyclopes; there is no agriculture, except for the wheat and vines that grow spontaneously, as they did in the mythical Golden Age; there is no practice of seafaring either, and consequently no crafts or trade. Although Polyphemus is a shepherd, who therefore knows how to look after his sheep and drinks milk, he nevertheless behaves like a savage: he drinks unmixed wine before, like a true anthropophage, swallowing two of Odysseus's companions. Moreover, Polyphemus recognises the authority of only one god, the violent Poseidon, thereby committing an act of *húbris* that, in a polytheistic regime, brings about the destruction of many figures in the heroic saga. He is compared to a wooded peak standing alone in the middle of the mountains, and thus has none of the sociability of "bread-eating" humans.[11] Similarly, in Odysseus's first contact with the Lotus-eaters who consume the fruit of forgetfulness, and in his anthropological approach to the anthropophagous Laestrygonians, his first question is whether they belong to the category of "bread-

---

[9] *Odyssey* 10, 1-12 and 10, 226-228.

[10] *Odyssey* 10, 118-120.

[11] *Odyssey* 9, 105-135 and 187-192. For more details on the figure of the Odyssean Cyclopes, see the studies by Pucci, 1998: 113-32 and Calame, 1985/2008.

eating" humans.[12]

It is thus through diet that the human is distinguished from other living beings belonging to the categories of the super- or sub-human; these beings of varying degrees of monstrosity, close to the animal realm, live in social and ecological environments corresponding to their qualities. By contrast, it is all the practices involved in making bread – from agricultural work to producing cereals and cooking flour – that define mortal humans as civilised beings. In addition, then, to the distinctly human cultural practices of the sharing of wine that has been duly mixed in the ritual symposium, generally under the aegis of Dionysus, and the sharing of meat at the end of the sacrificial act, which re-establishes in a ritual mode the communication of mortal men with the immortals, we can add the whole process of the agricultural production of wheat, the baking of bread, and the convivial consumption of cakes; the shared meal also features in cultic practices as a means for the communication of mortals with the gods.[13] Eating, as a cultural practice – which is a manifestation of Demeter's civilising effect on humans – involves not only *bíos*, that is, the material requirements for survival imposed by mortality, but also a practice of sociability, through the interactive communication of humans with both other humans and the gods, in an environment marked by these civilised practices.

As an *ánthrōpos*, and a mortal, the human being therefore has a "nature" whose developmental processes can only be realised in and through cultural practice.

2. *Phúsis, Nómos,* and the Environment

With such a processual definition, could the Greek *phúsis* be defined as "nature" in the context of an opposition – commonly used by the sophists – with *nómos*, the law? Can *phúsis* refer to the (dynamic)

---

[12] *Odyssey* 9, 82-97 and 10, 100-117.

[13] The definition of the civilisation of men by agricultural production and bloody sacrifice, which Ulysses implicitly claims during his journey, is the subject of the now classic study by Vidal-Naquet, 1970/1983. On the relation between the "ground wheat" conception of civilisation and the institution of sacrifice, see the excellent analysis by Vernant, 1979: 58-71.

"nature of things" in contrast with *nómos*, as "custom", "rule", instituted and shared by men? And can the Greek opposition between *phúsis* and *nómos* then be compared to the opposition that we modern are accustomed to make between "nature" and "culture"?

The famous aphorism of the materialist atomist Democritus comes to mind, which is quoted by the medical writer Galen on the subject of the impressions received by the senses: "By convention (*nómoi*) colour, by convention sweetness, by convention pungency; in reality, atoms and emptiness".[14] The final phrase begins, in Greek, with the word *eteêi* rather than *phúsei*, that is, "in reality" (in a form which, from Homeric poetry onwards, designates "what is") rather than "by nature". The opposition here is not between, on the one hand, the conventions and customs of humans and, on the other hand, the order of *phúsis*, but rather between appearances (for humans) and (physical) reality: in other words, not an opposition between culture and nature, but between appearances and reality. This opposition often appears in the thought of the Greek sages, and particularly Plato. As for the sophists, although they frequently use an opposition between *nómos* and *phúsis*, it extends only to the human domain, and is generally used to show the complementarity of the two processes.

It is probably the sophist Hippias, as presented to us by Plato in the *Protagoras*, who provides the most striking contrast between the concepts of *nómos* and *phúsis*. In an attempt to reconcile Protagoras and Socrates on the question of whether virtue is teachable or not (this is the theme of the dialogue), Hippias places great emphasis on the friendship and civic identity that binds the participants in the conversation: they can consider themselves as relatives, belonging to the same *génos*; they are *suggeneîs*, by "nature" (*phúsei*) and not by an effect of convention, of rule (*nómoi*). "Indeed", adds the sophist Hippias, portrayed by Plato, "by 'nature' [*phúsei*] like is related to like, whereas the 'law' [*nómos*], being a tyrant to men, generates much

---

[14] Democritus fr. 68 B 126 Diels-Kranz (=27.AtomD196 Laks-Most).

violence against 'nature'".[15]

While, in this passage of Plato's dialogue, *phúsis* certainly refers to the process of training of the sages assembled around Socrates in that prytaneum of knowledge that was Athens, the association of *nómos* with tyrannical power echoes Pindar's famous poetic fragment on "sovereign law".[16] Pindar's *nómos basileús* refers to the royal custom that dominates both mortals and immortals, and which can offend justice through its use of violence; this is demonstrated by some of the labours of Heracles, such as the steeling of the cattle of Geryon. It is this sense of *nómos*, designating a sovereign practice of a cultural order, that Herodotus uses in a famous scene in his *Histories*. The Persian king Darius, reflecting on the force of custom, questions certain representatives of other cultures regarding their contrasting funeral customs: on the one hand, Indians, who eat the corpses of their dead fathers, and on the other hand, Greeks, who burn their dead.[17] The conclusion to be drawn from this decentring of anthropological symmetry is self-evident: each people may reject with horror the customs instituted and practiced by others. But there is no question here of a *phúsis* (of humans), whether in opposition to or in collaboration with the that *nómos*-custom.

Let us return to the matter of human nature. In the view of the Hippocratic author of *On Ancient Medicine*, to question *phúsis*, as Empedocles does, was effectively to ask what it is to be a human being.[18] And there was no better perspective than that of the art of medicine for answering the question: "What is man?". In this Hippocratic conception of human nature, the human being is defined both by its development and by its constitution (the text speaks of "coagulation"). Good human constitution depends on a balanced process of "coction" and the correct mixture of humours and fundamental qualities (dry/wet, cold/hot). In this respect, diet is

---

[15] Plato, *Protagoras* 337cd.

[16] Pindar fr. 169a Maehler.

[17] Herodotus 3, 38, 4.

[18] Hippocrates, *On Ancient Medicine* 20, 1-3.

crucial; it is diet that determines the communication and interaction between man's internal organic system and, not "nature", but rather what we may call his environment. This anthropological representation of the human being, which applies to all humans regardless of gender or social status, is, strictly speaking, both "anthropopoietic" and "ecopoietic". Through its diet, the human's constitutive nature finds itself in an interactive and constrained relationship with the environment.

Another contemporary Hippocratic treatise, *On Airs, Waters, Places*, explicitly addresses the relationship between the physiological constitution of human beings and the corresponding qualities of the environment. The morphology and moral dispositions of human beings depend not only on variations in the organic mixture that makes up human nature, but also on the degree of exposure to the winds and the quality of the water in the cities they inhabit. Thus, in general, Europeans show more marked differences in their size and morphology than Asians do, since the former are subjected to a regime of more contrasting seasons in a harsher mountain environment.[19] Since, for Europeans, there are more frequently extreme variations in environmental conditions at the moment of the "coagulation" of the sperm in the formation of the embryo, they turn out to be savage, headstrong, independent, and courageous, whereas Asians, on the contrary, become gentle, indolent, submissive, or cowardly. According to this climatic conception of human nature, human beings, starting from a universally shared constitution, are led into series of ethnic and cultural differentiations.

Any such discussion of the relations between physiology and moral and cultural dispositions raises the possibility of an interaction between *phúsis* and *nómos*. This is the case, for example, of the Macrocephali, whose cranial morphology is caused by the cultural custom of shaping the heads of children by wrapping them in bands. But with time – according to *On Airs, Waters, Places* – the *nómos* was inscribed in "nature" (*en phúsei*), understood as a process of

---

[19] Hippocrates, *On Airs, Waters, Places* 12-13.

development. The custom thus ceased to exert its constraint, with the side effect that the particular morphology of the Macrocephali's elongated heads was weakened![20] Individual diets and shared cultural customs therefore contribute in a secondary way to the definition of an essentially processual human nature, which diversifies under the influence of the climate, and the interaction between the organic and the moral, the physical and the psychic. The ethnic and cultural communities that make up humankind are defined through this interaction between physical environment and human physiology, both of which are permeable because they are both based on the same qualities and are therefore subject, as *phúseis* (the plural of *phúsis*), to the same process of development.[21]

In the last chapter of the treatise, the Hippocratic author reinforces the contrast: in summary, those who live in a country with a temperate climate and abundant water have constitutions and characters that are "good", whereas those who live in dry regions subject to extreme seasonal changes have the most varied morphologies, characters, and "natures" (*phúsias*): hard, slender bodies, blond rather than black hair, confident and independent characters. Such differences in the "nature" of humans, in terms of their morphology and character, depend on the nature of the place, both through their diet and the water they drink: in both cases, the word used is *phúsis*. Finally, the author adds that humans living in a country with climatic extremes, "in such a nature", are more eager to work and more skilful and intelligent in the practice of the technical arts (*tékhnai*).[22] And I shall soon turn precisely to the uses that human beings make of these *tékhnai* in relation to their environment.

On the one hand, then, we find human nature conceived as physiology, morphology, and character in the making, and on the

---

[20] *On Airs, Waters, Places* 14, 1-5.

[21] This Hellenocentric image of the inhabited world, with Ionia, Athens, or Delos as its focal point, was widespread from the fifth century onwards. It is particularly present in the geography of Herodotus's *Histories*: see Calame, 1986/2005: 267-273.

[22] *On Airs, Waters, Places* 24, 5-10. See also the excellent commentary on this passage by Giorgianni, 2021: 126-133.

other, an environment envisaged as terrestrial space (both *gé* and *khóra*), a milieu whose climatic qualities also underpin the physiology of humans. Not nature and culture, but a dynamic and differentiated *phúsis* pertaining both to the environment and to the humans who inhabit it. Human beings draw from it the resources of their *bíos*, that is, the material means of their civilised survival as mortals. Between the *phúseis* of the places they inhabit and the *phúsis* of humans themselves, there is therefore a permeability and interaction, to which we will soon return. The environment and human beings organically share the same qualities.

Far from corresponding to the modern division between nature and culture, the sometimes contrasting collaboration between *phúsis* and *nómos* more closely resembles the modern distinction between the innate and the acquired: on the one hand, that which is given by a nature governed by a principle of generation and development (in a given ecology); and on the other hand, that which is accepted and consequently practised by the communities of humans, especially through the effect of education. In this respect, we should recall the observation made by the rhetorician and sophist Antiphon, in a fragment (only recently reconstituted) of the treatise *On Truth*: "We understand and respect [the customs] of our neighbours, but not those of people who live far away. In so doing, we make ourselves barbarians to one another, for by nature [*phúsei*] we were begotten [*pephúkamen*] to be barbarians as well as Greeks".[23]

3. Hellenic Forms of Practical and Interpretative Intelligence

However, besides this physiological and moral conception of mortal humans, conceived in terms of the humoral and qualitative composition of their organism in relation to their geo-terrestrial and climatic environment, another attempt at defining the human was made by the *sophoí* preceding Socrates who addressed the subject of *phúsis*.[24] In his treatise on the parts of animals, Aristotle considers the

---

[23] Antiphon fr. 44 Pendrick, with the commentary provided by Thomas, 2000:102-134, on the dialectic between *nómos* and *phúsis* in the anthropology of the Classical era.

[24] See Vegetti, 1987: 95-116 for citations and a good commentary of the numerous attestations of these

relationship between the intelligence that is characteristic of humans and the use that they make of their hands as instruments. In this regard, Aristotle cites Anaxagoras of Clazomena; for this contemporary of the sophists in the Athens of Pericles, it is their hands that make humans the most intelligent (*phronimótatos*) of animals. He adds that it is in fact humans' intelligence that allows them to use their hands: "It is therefore to the being that is capable of acquiring the greatest number of technical arts [*tékhnai*] that nature [*hē phúsis*] has given hands, by far the most useful of tools".[25] Consequently, when we speak of human hands we are speaking of an *órganon* conceived both as an organ and as an instrument, and when we speak of an *órganon* we are therefore also speaking of technical instruments. We shall return to this too.

While Anaxagoras defined the practical intelligence that characterises humans in terms of *phroneîn*, that is as prudent reflection based on right feeling and presence of mind, his contemporary Alcmaeon of Croton defined the human being in relation to its capacity for understanding (*súnesis*): unlike other animate beings who perceive without understanding, the human "grasps" (*xuníesi*).[26] On this basis, the human would be distinguished from animals by the practical intelligence that is *súnesis* (and not by the wisdom of craftmanship or cunning skill that is *mêtis*!). For another contemporary, the historiographer Thucydides, this form of intelligence (*súnesis*) is the distinguishing feature of great Athenian politicians such as Themistocles or Pericles, or even of the tutelary hero of Athens, Theseus himself.

The human being, which is itself an animal, is therefore differentiated from other living beings by two specific abilities: a technical

---

"pre-Socratic" conceptions of the essence of man; by way of comparison, see also Lloyd, 2012: 8-30.

[25] Anaxagoras fr. 59 A 102 Diels-Kranz (= 25. Anaxag. D80 Laks-Most), quoted by Aristotle, *Parts of Animals* 10, 687a 6-23. On the representations of the human hand from Aristotle to Galen, see the study by Longo, 2000.

[26] Alcméon fr. 24 A 5 and B 1 a Diels-Kranz (=23. Alcm. D11 Laks-Most), in fragments quoted by Theophrastus, *On the Senses* 25-26. Longo, 1995, has reviewed these definitions of the human in relation to different forms of a practical intelligence that does not necessarily correspond to the artisanal intelligence of *mêtis*!

intelligence exercised with the help of an organ such as the hand and with the use of various "technical arts", and a political intelligence of a moral and social nature. It is the combination of these two types of practical intelligence that makes it possible to live as a society, which characterises what we would call the civilisation of mortal humans, or simply culture. Heraclitus attributes to humans a faculty of *tó phroneîn*, understood as an attitude and judgement that are both prudent and wise, stating that "it has been given to all men to know themselves and to think wisely [*sophroneîn*]".[27] In Delphic wisdom it is this *sophroneîn*, as wise moderation, that allows humans, with self-knowledge, not to exceed the limits assigned to their mortal condition. This is why, adds Heraclitus, "wise moderation is the greatest of virtues, and wisdom [*sophíe*] consists in speaking the truth and acting according to nature [*katà phúsin*] by listening to it".[28] Through shared wisdom, the culture of mortal humans, in a universal way, would thus involve listening to "nature".

This philosophical conception of the human as a civilised animal is not only based on the universal sharing of intellectual qualities allowing, on the one hand, productive technical acts and, on the other hand, balanced social relations; this cultural "humanism" is also based on a shared capacity to perceive one's environment as intelligible, and to understand it by means of the interpretative arts, which consist in the reading of signs. To use an example from another Hippocratic treatise, it is a hermeneutic principle of semiotics that underlies the process of medical prognosis. Indeed, the author of the *Prognostics*, a work devoted to the doctor's ability to see the patient's past, present, and future, states in the conclusion of the treatise that:

> *It is necessary to know this about the marks of proof* [tekméria] *and other signs* [semeîa], *and not to overlook that, every year, in every*

---

[27] Heraclitus fr. 22 B 113 and 116 Diels-Kranz (= 9. Her. D29-30 Laks-Most).

[28] Fr. 22 B 112 Diels-Kranz (=9. Her D114a-b Laks-Most). Kahn, 1979: 14-23 and 116-123 shows that Heraclitus ultimately founds law and political order on the *lógos*, understood as discourse, as well as on the *noûs*, understood as understanding; for the idea of the human race in the Sophists, and then in Plato, see Baldry, 1965: 35-45 and 72-87.

season, bad signs indicate something bad and good ones something good;
indeed, the listed signs turn out to tell the truth, whether in Libya, Delos,
or Scythia.[29]

Note that, from a geographical point of view, this definition of the
spatial extent of the applicability of Greek semiotic art reveals the
ambivalent character of its apparent universality. In fact, the apparent
universal validity of the medical interpretation of symptoms is
inscribed in a representation of the inhabited world which, from the
extreme regions of the Libyan south and the Scythian north, is
centred on the island of Delos; this is the religious and economic
centre of an Aegean Sea dominated, in Classical times, by the city of
Athens.[30] Given the universal nature of human physiology, the
"nature" (*phúsis*) of diseases lends itself to a semiotic reading, focused
on the particular case, regardless of geo-terrestrial and climatic
variations.

4. Prometheus and Semiotic Practices

These semiotic arts, developed in particular by Greek doctors, now
bring us back to the *tékhnai* – the sort technical knowledge that,
according to myth, Prometheus transmitted to humans. In his role as
the benefactor of mortal humans, Prometheus is notably portrayed
in the play *Prometheus Bound* by Aeschylus (or one of his contemporary
tragic poets, since the authorship is disputed) a little before the
dissemination of the first Hippocratic treaties.

From as early as the composition of the *Iliad*, *tékhnē* corresponded to
the art of the craftsman. When Hector, the indefatigable warrior,
takes Paris to task for his dedication to the zither and the gifts of
Aphrodite, Paris responds by comparing Hector's unyielding heart
to an axe in the hands of a carpenter hewing a ship's hull.[31] In Plato's
Gorgias, the speakers try to define the rhetorical art by comparing it

---

[29] Hippocrates, *Prognosticon* 25, 3; cf. 1, 1.

[30] On the Athenocentric representation of the inhabited world, which notably informs the Hippocratic
treatise *On Airs, Waters, Places*, see note 25.

[31] *Iliad* 3, 59-64.

successively to the art of weaving for the manufacture of fabrics, to the art of the Muses for the creation of songs, to gymnastics for the appropriate constitution of the body, to medicine for understanding and explaining the ills of the sick, and then to painting, sculpture, and many other crafts: in short, a wide range of technical arts viewed as artisanal practices and work (*ergasía*), but also as discourse (*lógos*), as in the case of poetry and speech.[32] And so the rhetorical art is naturally included in this category, since, like arithmetic or geometry, it acts through speech. The difference between these technical arts, all of which depend on the practical intelligence of the human being, lies in their object.

But there is more than this to the nature and effect of the practice of such technical arts. In a famous scene, Aeschylus's Prometheus, chained to a rock in a deserted wilderness at the northern edge of the inhabited world, describes the animal state to which mortals were originally condemned. Living underground like ants, humans looked without seeing, and listened without hearing. In order to bring them out of their primal state, in which humans were unable to use their senses, the civilising hero invented and taught them a series of skills and practical arts: the observation of the rising and setting of the stars as a way of organising work in the fields; mnemonic arts such as arithmetic and writing, which is the "memory of all things"; the techniques of domesticating animals for agriculture and trade; the many recipes for medicines in order to free oneself from diseases; the various arts of divination, including the interpretation of dreams, the hermeneutics of double-meaning words, the interpretation of the flight and habits of birds and the viscera of sacrificed animals; and, above all, the gift of fire, that "master [*didáskalos*] of all arts [*tékhnes*]", as Prometheus states at the start of the tragedy, claiming that it is a great means to advance beyond an impasse (*póros*). He adds that, by means of fire, humans will learn "many arts [*tékhnai*]"; it is notably essential for producing iron from the mineral resources of the earth

---

[32] Plato, *Gorgias* 449c-450e. For a definition of the lexical and semantic field of *tékhne*, see the study by Warin, 2021.

by means of craftsmanship.[33]

These *tékhnai*, corresponding to know-how in the order of technical and artisanal skill, are successively presented by Prometheus as artifices (*sophísmata*), ingenious means (*mechanémata*), and as expedients (*póroi*) enabling all humans to get out of a difficult situation. Certainly, this technical knowledge pertains to the artisanal intelligence which, in Athens, was overseen by the blacksmith god Hephaestus and the perceptive Athena; it depends on *mêtis*, the ingenious, cunning, and astute intelligence that the Greeks – in their own self-perception – embodied.[34] Yet, beyond the skill of the craftsman, all the forms of knowledge invented by Prometheus correspond to the ability to read systems of signs. They depend on the practical intelligence that, over and above the artisan's intelligence, allows mortal humans to understand, reflect, and interpret.[35]

Since the practical arts, the *tékhnai*, are of a semiotic order, it therefore follows that the environment of the human being is constituted as a system of signs. *Phúsis*, understood as "nature" in the process of becoming but also as the living environment of mortal human beings, is something to be deciphered by means of the arts of interpretation, which lead either to practices that ensure survival, or to the prediction of a future whose general direction does not depend on humans. The semiotic and hermeneutic techniques of Aeschylus's Prometheus thus enable humans to ensure their own survival in a changing and signifying environment; but this is a way of life constrained by the limits of a mortal and unpredictable condition, subject to many twists of fate.

Just as with Descartes, the perspective outlined here is a positively utilitarian one. The Promethean techniques, based on the reading of

---

[33] Aeschylus, *Prometheus Bound* 109-113, 248-256, and 436-506. For details, see Calame, 2010: 36-48. On the relationship between Greek conceptions of the technical arts, as imagined through the figure of Prometheus, and the modern concept of work, see Vernant, 1966.

[34] See Detienne & Vernant, 1974: 176-200.

[35] See references collected in Calame, 2008: 44-46.

"nature", or rather of an environment to be interpreted as a dynamic system of signs, are presented as *ophelémata*: "advantages", sources of profit. They are characterised by their social utility. By means of foresighted deciphering and artisanal intelligence, they make civilised life possible for mortals; but with the danger pointed out by the chorus of Sophocles's *Antigone*: the use of *tékhnai* can lead man to act in ways that are either good or evil, including in the context of the pólis.[36] When Plato reformulates and repurposes this episode from the heroic legend of Prometheus in the *Protagoras*, he emphasises this principle of social unity that is present in technical practices; he presents them as a *politikè tékhne*, political art and civic justice, which he conceives as a gift from Zeus to mortals.[37] However, unlike for Descartes, the environment is here something to be deciphered and interpreted, since it constitutes a semiotic whole; it is therefore not instituted as an objectified nature, to be dominated by human reason.

The interpretative skills invented and taught by Aeschylus's Prometheus thus enable humans to use their sensory capacities in relation to their environment. Thanks to their senses, coupled with a practical and reflective intelligence, human beings can make their environment into a meaningful world. Prometheus, chained to a rock at the northern edge of the inhabited earth, but simultaneously present on the Attic stage in front of an Athenian audience, expresses himself, in opposition to the dominating power of Zeus, somewhat like a forerunner of the sophists; he offers mortal humans the sort of hermeneutic practices that could only be conceived by the Athenians of the fifth century, who were such masters of the interpretation of oracles and double-meaning narratives.[38]

The various technical arts invented by the Prometheus of the Attic tragedy bring humans out of an initial state of blindness (and therefore incompleteness) by granting them an interpretative

---

[36] Sophocles, *Antigone* 353-75. See my short commentary, the last part of the foreword to this essay, and the comment by Giorgianni, 2016: 144-145.

[37] Plato, *Protagoras* 320c-323a. On this Platonic use of the "myth" of Prometheus, see Morgan, 2000: 132-154, and my own study of 2012.

[38] See Said, 1975: 131-187, and Cerri, 1975: 45-53.

clairvoyance, and thereby leading them to a specifically human state of civilisation. The culture of mortal humans causes them to interact with a "nature" which, as a signifying system, can be shaped by practical intelligence and techniques, to the benefit of human society.

II

FROM THE ENLIGHTENMENT PHILOSOPHERS
TO MODERN ANTHROPOLOGISTS

Let us now return to the European opposition between nature and culture, as enshrined by Descartes and the Enlightenment philosophers: a nature subject to mechanical and physical laws and a culture founded on reason, which is universally and exclusively possessed by humans. In the passage quoted earlier from Lévi-Strauss himself,[1] the contrast between nature and culture shifts to a more cautious opposition between "animality" and "humanity", or an animal nature and human nature. He notes that, in cultures marked by "savage thought", the contrast between nature and culture is generally neither relevant nor operative. In this respect, the anthropologist who founded structuralism and promoted binary oppositions showed himself to be open to a certain cultural relativism.

It is surely no coincidence that, in the middle of the eighteenth century, when Buffon returned to the question of the relationship between man and nature, he did so not only in terms reminiscent of Hippocratic thought, but also by establishing a strong opposition between human and animal. The fifteen volumes of *L'Histoire naturelle, générale et particulière* (published in Paris between 1749 and 1778) are the result of a long undertaking to classify the animal species that Europeans had come to know through their travels and conquests across all the continents of the world. He placed humans at the top of this vast animal taxonomy. Among all living beings, only the human being has an immaterial soul; it is the seat of thought, which humans alone are capable of communicating through speech. In opposition to those who suggested that man was descended from

---

[1] Lévi-Strauss, 1973/1978: 320.

apes through a series of successive differentiations, he argued that "there is more than enough here to demonstrate the excellence of our nature and the huge distance that the Creator has placed between man and beast; man is a reasonable being, the animal is a being without reason" – this is the conclusion that Buffon draws from his introductory reflections in the volume specifically devoted to the "natural history" of man.[2]

The nature of man is given as universal, and the different "races" represent only varieties of the human species. These differences between humans, who share a fundamentally homogeneous nature, can be explained by the influence of the climate, with its various parameters, which inscribes certain morphological features in the hereditary lineage. Conversely, the degree of civilisation exhibited by each of the different human groups depends on man's action on his natural environment. Thus the climate determines the variations in man's nature, but human beings, as they proliferated and grew in power, were no longer content merely to interpret nature, as the humans instructed by Prometheus had done; they now also transformed their environment by subjecting the empire of nature to their technical skill.

Accordingly, Buffon characterises the seventh and final "era of Nature" as that in which "the power of Man came to rival that of Nature". In conclusion, he declares that:

> *Man only belatedly came to know the extent of his power [...]; it depends entirely on the exercise of his intelligence; thus the more he observes, the more he cultivates Nature, and the more means he has to subdue her and the more possibilities to draw from her bosom new riches, without diminishing the treasures of her inexhaustible fertility.*[3]

Consequently, in the interaction between man and his environment, human reason is the determining factor, which not only models, but also exploits for man's benefit a nature that is modified by his action

---

[2] Buffon, 1774: 171.

[3] Buffon, 1780: II, 209-210. See Duchet, 1995: 229-280.

and of which he himself is a part.

We will soon return to the consequences of this civilising action of man on a "Nature" that has been dignified with the use of a capital letter, and consequently personified.

1. Anthropology Avant la Lettre

In fact, from the Renaissance onwards, colonial expansion brought Christian Europeans, now steeped in Greco-Roman culture, into contact with communities of "savages", who were immediately identified with the origins of humanity. This gave rise, at the very moment of the Enlightenment, to a remarkable expansion of reflection on the universal nature of man and the diversity of cultures.

For missionary theologians such as the Jesuit Father Joseph-François Lafitau, the claimed unity of humanity derived from its unique Adamic origin. The variety of cultures is then seen as a consequence of the immigration of peoples from the place of God's creation and the gradual degradation of a primitive religious feeling, before the unifying and civilising enterprise of Christianity intervened. However, the contributors to the *Encyclopédie* replaced the idea of a created human nature with the concept of a human animal endowed with thought and sociability, who is confronted with a physical nature subject to the mechanistic laws of motion intended by God. This is a conception of man characterised by his use of speech, who, at the centre of the world – and far removed from the divine project imagined by Jean-Jacques Rousseau – shapes this world to his own use; a civil man whose arts and sciences can impose the civilising action of the "natural man" against the deviances of an artificial and degraded morality. As mentioned above, man now shapes the nature, or milieu, that forms his living environment.

Moreover, in response to the Enlightenment conception of the universal civilisation of man, which soon came to be understood as the "culture of humanity", Johann Gottfried Herder and the German Romantics formulated an understanding of culture both as education

(*Bildung*) and as the expression of the genius of a particular people. On the one hand, then, culture is seen as a form of training that makes it possible to fill the gaps in a man who is naturally lacking, a man who is incomplete in his phylogenesis and ontogenesis, a man marked by an incompleteness that is constitutive of human nature. Thus, after affirming that "our distinctive characteristic [is] that we are almost devoid of instinct, and that we are formed into humanity only by the practice of life as a whole", Herder clarifies that:

> the education [Bildung] of our species is twofold; it is original in so far as it is communicated, and organic in so far as what is communicated is received and applied. It matters little whether we call this second creation culture [Kultur], in reference to the action of cultivating the soil, or whether we say that man is enlightened, borrowing this expression from the phenomenon of light; the chain of light and culture extends to the ends of the earth.[4]

On the other hand, this same culture is represented as the multiform and differentiated expression of the spirit and soul of a people that has become a nation: these range from the first forms of *Zivilisation* represented by primitive peoples to the *Kultur* of the great peoples devoted to the religion of the book (that is, the Bible). Or, alternatively, we are invited to see a passage from *Hochkulturen* to the decay of civilisation, in Oswald Spengler's narrative leading to the need to institute Prussian socialism...[5]

We should note – making a brief return to Classical Greece – that one of the earliest of the pre-Platonic sages mentioned above seems to have been the first to emphasise the role played by education in the making of the human being. According to a treatise attributed to Plutarch that summarises the thought of Anaximander of Miletus, the latter asserted that "from the beginning the human was

---

[4] Herder, 1784/1989: 336-345 (II, book 9, ch. 1). This chapter is, significantly, entitled "However willing man may be to imagine that he produces everything from himself, he is nevertheless subject to the influence of external nature in the development of his faculties"! In response to the human being's essential incompleteness, we refer to the "anthropo-poietic" approach opened up by Remotti, 1999: 21-23 (= 2013: 40-43), to which we will return; see the references given in relation to this subject in chap. III note 9.

[5] See on this subject the good perspective proposed by Cuche, 1996: 10-14,

distinguished from living beings of a different appearance in that other animate beings quickly take on an autonomous life, whereas humans require long-term educational care".[6] By starting from the implicit idea that the specificity of the human being lies in a constitutive lack of autonomy, Anaximander seems to anticipate the process described and developed twenty-five centuries later by Herder, leading to the conclusion: man is nothing without *Bildung*, and nothing without *Kultur*!

Whatever the relationship between these two instances might be – and there is no suggestion here of genealogy – the spiritual dimension conferred by Herder on human cultures laid the foundation for the crucial distinction that was established over the course of the nineteenth century between *Naturwissenschaft* and *Geisteswissenschaften*: natural sciences on one side, human sciences on the other. We shall return to this modern paradigm, which we have approached here via a critical detour through Classical Greece and the Enlightenment, and address the consequences that have arisen from its particular division in the contemporary period.

2. Global Definitions of Human Culture

How, then, has the other pole of this binarism been conceived, that of a culture placed in opposition to a nature-object?

> *Culture or civilisation, taken in its wide ethnological sense, is that complex whole which includes knowledge, belief, art, morals, law, custom, and any other capabilities or habits acquired by man as a member of society.*[7]

Such is the first properly anthropological definition of culture, as it is given in Edward B. Tylor's study of *Primitive Culture*. This comprehensive conception encompasses all aspects of man's social life, including the practices that Pierre Bourdieu would later trace

---

[6] Anaximander fr. 12 A 10 Diels-Kranz (= 6. Anaximand. D8 Laks-Most). We refer again to the numerous attestations of these "pre-Socratic" conceptions of the essence of man cited and well commented by Vegetti, 1987: 95-116.

[7] Tylor, 1871: I, 1. Emphasis ours.

back to *habitus*. We could easily include in it what Herodotus's Darius understood under the term *nómoi*, as well as the technical arts invented by Aeschylus's Prometheus. This conception, descended from the universalism of the Enlightenment, is based on the unity of a human race whose cultures evolve from the most primitive to the most developed, from the most "natural" (*die Natuvölker...*) to the most "civilised", in a line that is diverse enough to allow for a certain relativism.[8]

From an anthropological point of view, culture, as a structuring style of life in society, is transmissible, and is also the distinctive feature of human communities; the differences that mark these communities are not biological, but are based on convention and the acquired. There are, however, two major differences from conceptions of culture found in Classical Greece: on the one hand, in this first modern definition of culture, the different states of culture are inscribed in a line which, with some qualifications, leads from the natural to the civilised; on the other hand, as an autonomous set of social phenomena specific to a given people, culture is cut off from nature.

The social concept of a human culture that encompasses the diversity of cultures of human communities, while setting apart a nature that is posited in opposition to man, became particularly entrenched in Francophone anthropology. This concept of culture is the basis of Émile Durkheim's thinking, and then of Marcel Mauss's work on the non-linear evolution and differences presented by the examples of different "civilisations", based on a general notion of civilisations of "variable geometry". According to such a conception, cultures, corresponding to elementary forms, are driven less by human reason than by "collective representations", constituting for each people a "collective consciousness". Whether or not one agrees with

---

[8] Following others, Kilani (2009: 211-228) emphasises the context of colonial domination in which nineteenth-century European anthropologists traced this evolutionary and unidirectional line from the primitive to the civilised. This model, combined with Hegelian idealism, also influenced the conception of human history developed by Marx and Engels, leading from primitive communities, through slavery-based and feudal societies, to capitalist society.

Durkheim's distinction between political and social institutions on the one hand, and manifestations of culture on the other, one will recognise the conclusion that he comes to in his well-known essay "Note sur la notion de civilisation" ("Note on the Concept of Civilisation"):

> *Political and legal institutions as well as phenomena of social morphology form part of the specific make-up of each people. In contrast, myths, tales, money, commerce, fine arts, techniques, tools, languages, words, scientific knowledge, literary forms and ideals – all these travel and are borrowed, and therefore result from a history broader than that of a single society.*[9]

There is therefore no *Naturvölker*, and no people "without civilisation". Yet this sociological perspective implicitly omits any questioning either of human nature or of the "natural" environment in which it develops. In short, it is as if human societies had always already existed.

Nevertheless, the functionalist anthropology developed by Bronisław Malinowski would later reinstate a crucial role for human nature, in relation to a diversified environment, by postulating that humans have a range of primary, universal, and pre-cultural needs. Malinowski, who devoted much of his studies to an ethnology of the inhabitants of the Trobriand Islands, describes culture as "the integral whole consisting of implements and consumer goods, of constitutional charters for the various social groupings, of human ideas and crafts, beliefs and customs".[10] Culture thus becomes the institutional response of each individual community to the functional imperatives arising from man's biological requirements in a certain living environment: in other words, cultural responses (subsistence, kinship, shelter, protection, education, hygiene) to basic needs (metabolism, reproduction, security, movement, growth, health). Just

---

[9] Durkheim & Mauss, 1913/2009: 38. See also, in the same essay: "While there does not exist a single human civilisation, there have always been a diversity of civilisations which dominate and surround the collective life specific to each people" (p. 38). On the forms taken by the notion of culture among the founders of French ethnology, see, for example, Cuche, 1996: 22-29; for the form that this notion took in dialogue with American anthropologists, see Dianteill, 2012: 95-109.

[10] Malinowski, 1944/1961: 36.

as for Herder, education here plays an essential role in "the gradual teaching of the skills of knowledge, custom, and moral principles" that underpin all culture, to a much greater extent than in animals.

In this pragmatic perspective, human nature makes a spectacular comeback as the functional premise underlying all the cultural of a given human group. These human activities are embedded in an organic whole, made up of institutions that control economic, moral, and ritual practices, and are endowed with a kind of sociological intentionality.

Human nature thus came to be reintegrated in the field of anthropology. But what about nature in the sense of the environment that is indispensable to every human being for its survival?

3. The Reintegration of Nature and Symbolic Practices

From the middle of the twentieth century onwards, cultural and social anthropology drew its structuralist inspiration from modern thinking on the functioning of linguistic and semiotic systems. From this point on, nature has featured in the discourse of anthropology on the configurations and functions of culture. Lévi-Strauss's hypothesis on the elementary structures of kinship had a major influence on this development.[11] In his view, the natural and universal function of reproduction, which is the very essence of the human being, is, for humans, the object of structuring rules that belong to the relative order of culture; these rules can be traced back to the universal norm that prohibits incest. By extension, he suggests that "everything universal in man relates to the natural order, and is characterized by spontaneity, and that everything subject to a norm is cultural and is both relative and particular".[12]

This implicit return to the Greek opposition between *phúsis* and *nómos*, or to the modern distinction between the innate and the acquired (including the principle of complementarity between these

---

[11] Lévi-Strauss, 1969: 3-10.

[12] Lévi-Strauss, 1969: 8.

two concepts), was also accompanied by a break with the evolutionary paradigm of a progressive movement from nature to culture: man would not be man if he could not from the outset express himself in a culture, in the regulated and symbolic (I would say, by anticipation, "anthropopoietic") construction and transformation of his own nature. For the rules of kinship, stemming from the prohibition of incest, function as a semiotic system of communication that informs the social and symbolic structures of the community: in other words, we are faced here with the nature of man in his procreative faculty, and with culture as a system of kinship. The nature of the structuralist anthropologists, understood as human nature, is far removed from the physical nature of the Enlightenment authors of the *Encyclopédie*.

We have therefore passed from a model based on the advancement of the Mind and Reason towards civility, starting from a state of nature in which early, savage man is dominated by his animal instincts, to a model based on rules of a cultural order; these rules are inscribed in the very nature of man, or even in the unconscious structures of the human mind.[13] The human thus becomes human through culture. Moreover, away from any structural canonisation of the opposition between nature and culture, it turns out that every society produces its own representation of a culture that prevails over nature and that distinguishes, for example, man from animal. The opposition between nature and culture can then only be valid as an operative concept.

To the precise extent that the structural contrast between nature and culture becomes instrumental (and therefore relative), it now makes it possible to address the different symbolic modes in which human communities envisage their relationship with nature, now understood as a milieu indispensable to man's survival. On the one

---

[13] The stages of this supposed passage of man from a savage nature to the enlightenment of reason have been traced by Duchet, 1995: 322-376. Let us recall that Rousseau reverses these values when he states, in the conclusion to his *Discours sur l'origine et les fondements de l'inégalité parmi les hommes* ("*Discourse on the Origin and Foundations of Inequality among Men*"): "It is enough for me to have proved that this is not the original state of man, and that this is only the spirit of society, and the inequality that society engenders, which thus change and alter all our natural inclinations" (1755/1992: 70).

hand, then, there is a culture manifested in the systems of exchange of women, goods, and messages, whether verbal or iconic – in short, a culture manifested in practico-symbolic communication. On the other hand, there is a nature-environment, a nature-milieu, which, as in the Hippocratic treatise *On Airs, Waters, Places*, varies from one community to another, a nature-milieu that seems to be fundamentally permeable to the practical and speculative work of culture.

III

BEYOND ANTHROPOLOGICAL DETERMINISMS: PERMEABILITIES

Modern social and cultural anthropology, having adopted a structuralist model and become focused on the symbolic, has devoted its attention to the representations made in other communities of the interaction between nature and culture; this project brings with it the temptation to naturalise what is merely an operative opposition, and the risk of projecting this dualism, based on an "etic" conception (implicitly given as universal), onto the "emic" (and native) categories. In fact, indigenous anthropologies, much like the Hippocratic system, integrate the human being and its "natural" environment into a homogeneous system. This system is permeated and driven by forces – often represented in an anthropomorphic way – that affect both human beings and their environment. These conceptions and representations are characterised by the permeability between orders, precisely where Western thought has endeavoured to construct more rigid distinctions: the physical, the biological, the animal, the human, the divine, etc. We will return to this in order to consider the possible existence of four distinct "ontologies" that would conceive of human beings' relationship with their environment, each of them transcending an opposition between nature and culture.

1. There Is No Human without Culture

However, for the moment, and before undertaking a critique of the opposition between nature and culture through the lens of contemporary science, let us briefly mention a significant aspect of humans' relationship with their environment: namely, their relationship – perceived as both natural and cultural – with the animal world.

In fact, we have recently witnessed attempts – in fields as diverse as sociobiology, Marxist anthropology, cultural ecology, and animal ethology, each reflecting on their own particular aspects of the life of humans in society – to readdress the old question of the influence of the physical, biological, and social environment on human cultural behaviour. On the implicit premise of a unidirectional determinism, manifestations of culture are readily seen as adaptive responses: responses to a particular geographical and climatic ecology; responses to innate biological mechanisms characterising either the human species or individuals in their singularity; and responses to particular economic and social relationships and systems. Yet the cultural manifestations of humans are also seen as expressions of animal behavioural patterns, and are thus inscribed in a paradigm of biological determinism of human behaviour.

Anthropological work in the field of animal ethology has often criticised the anthropomorphism underlying the investigation of animal behaviour as the basis for human behaviour. In fact, recent approaches, which have previously been marked by an attitude of behaviourist determinism, show that the relationship between humans and animals should be reconsidered in light of the considerable plasticity of animal behaviour. Indeed, it appears that some animals tend to modify their "ritual" gestures when they enter into contact with humans.[1] Evidently, anthropological enquiry cannot assume a position of neutrality even when studying animals, as the relationship still proves to be an interactive one, influencing the behaviour of both the interviewer and the interviewee!

This sort of humanisation of the relationship between humans and animals shows not only that the relationship between humans, animals, and nature can only be thought of in dialectical terms of interaction (indeed, just like the ethnological relationship between humans and other humans), but also that the human-animal-nature relationship (again, like the human-human relationship) is necessarily anthropocentric, and therefore asymmetrical: the interpretation of

[1] Lestel, 2003: 387-407.

the behaviour of animal societies in cultural terms is the work of humans. The humanisation of the animal is then complemented by an interactive animalisation of human culture.[2] Just as human constructs animal society, on the basis of their own observations and perceptions, so they reconstruct themselves through the animal.

However, beyond the relations of each human community with a particular physical ecology and animal environment, beyond their representations of these different relations, and beyond the discourses that disseminate those representations, recent research, in both genetic biology and neural sciences, has once again focused attention on the "nature" of human beings. Just as in the Classical Athens of the sophists, the matter now at hand is the development of the practical and intellectual capacities of the human species in the diversity of its communities, both from the phylogenetic perspective, bearing on the development of the human species, and from the ontogenetic perspective, bearing on the development of each individual.

Taking an anthropological approach to the question, it seems that the processes of neural, and thus mental development of humans in their collective history depend both on innate and inherited mechanisms and on the cultural resources that are available, in interaction with different ecosystems. There is therefore no basic human nature, no purely innate, biological constitution of the human being; but neither is there an ontology of the human as a thinking being, and therefore of the human of culture.

On the one hand, the human being, in its native incompleteness, and by virtue of this constitutive incompleteness, develops through culture and through the exercise of that culture, and this is true both in terms of the history of the species and in terms of the development of individuals. All culture works gradually to make up for the incompleteness that is so marked in human beings that it constitutes one of their distinctive features. On the other hand, and as if in

---

[2] See in this regard the well-reasoned conclusions of Rivera, 1999: 65-70.

reverse, culture is a prerequisite for the development of human thought. The human being's extraordinary mental capacities cannot develop without the work of culture, which involves interaction with the environment. Indeed, technical practices such as hunting, the use of fire, and the making of tools, as well as symbolic practices accomplished through gesture and language, in myth, ritual, art, religion, and finally science, have gradually shaped the human organism (and, I would add, the neuronal potential of human brains), to the point of becoming indispensable, not only for humans' survival, but also for their "existential realisation":

> *We are, in sum, incomplete or unfinished animals who complete or finish ourselves through culture – and not through culture in general but through highly particular forms of it.*[3]

From this, the American anthropologist Marshall Sahlins concludes that "culture is the human nature", and goes on to assert, based on Marx, that human beings, "born neither good nor bad, [...] make themselves in social activity as it unfolds in given historical circumstances", with the qualification that those "given historical circumstances" should be replaced by "given cultural orders".[4]

In short, echoing the account of the development of the human species provided by the tragic Prometheus, as portrayed by Aeschylus on the Attic stage, we can state the situation as follows: just as there is no culture without the human, there is no human without culture!

It is probably unhelpful, in our understanding of the interaction between the human of culture and its environment, to apply the metaphor of the text to any and all cultural systems; we would then pass from the idea of the "book of nature" to that of the "book of culture"... Instead of the environment being configured such as to

---

[3] This is the judgement of the anthropologist Clifford Geertz (1973: 33-54 and 55-83), in two successive essays entitled "The Impact of the Concept of Culture on the Concept of Man" (1966) and "The Growth of Culture and the Evolution of Mind" (1962) respectively (1973: 49 for the quotation); see the commentary on this in Calame, 2010: 76-79.

[4] Sahlins, 2009: 109-110.

be read like a book, human cultures would instead be approached in this way. When the metaphor of the text is applied either to the idea of nature or to that of culture (and indeed when it is applied to the human genome and to genetic engineering), it entails the illusion of a deterministic form of decoding. However, just as with the divinatory arts taught by Prometheus to mortal humans, the "reading" of the environment, as well as that of human practices, not to mention the reading of humans' cultural and symbolic productions, is necessarily interpretative. For meaning does not reside in things, nor indeed in texts, as a supposedly critical philology would have us believe; rather, meaning is always a matter of effect (semantics) and of the representations that we produce, based on our perceptions and the questions that we bring to these things or texts. The fact that we now have an empirical grasp of both the organisms that make up our milieu and our own organism as human beings, in terms of physics, chemistry, and biology, is due to the use of logico-mathematical models and computational tools that are themselves products of the human brain (with its basis in neural networks) and human intellect!

We can therefore readily endorse the conclusion that an anthropologist of symbolic ecologies (to whom we will soon will return) draws from an investigation of the ways in which different cultures construct "nature" in the relationships established between humans and non-humans:

> Going beyond universalism and relativism implies ceasing to treat society and culture, as well as human faculties and physical nature, like autonomous substances, thus opening the way to a true ecological understanding of the constitution of individual and collective entities. [...] the entities of which our universe is made have a meaning and identity solely through the relations that constitute them as such.[5]

---

[5] Descola, 1996: 98-99.

2. Biological Porosities and Neuronal Interactions: Between Nature and Culture

The "nature" of the human being is therefore made through its interaction with its physical, vegetal, and animal environment, and is unmade by the very exercise of the human's perceptive, practical, affective, mental (we would now say "neuronal"), interpretative, and psychic abilities. The human being, in its mortal condition, creates and destroys itself in an interactive relationship, of both constructive and destructive continuity, with the ecosystem from which it draws its indispensable resources, and with the social environment that sustains its fleeting survival as an individual person. In this interaction on the ecological and sociological level, in the order of meaning, each individual human, through their practices and mental activities, contributes to shaping and reshaping (undoubtedly this also functions in the genetic domain) both their environment and the species to which they belong; these practices and intellectual activities rely on and produce cultural representations that are always differentiated, both individually and collectively.

The dichotomy between "us" and "others" – another form of opposition favoured by anthropological thought in the structuralist tradition – is in danger of suffering the same fate, since it is based on an implicit conception of cultures as closed systems. This opposition, enshrined by the use of a capital letter to refer to "the Other", has led to the naturalisation of "nationalist identities" and the postulation of "clashes" between civilisations that are in fact close neighbours. Indeed, what could be closer than Christianity and Islam – two hegemonic and proselytising monotheisms, based on a revealed truth recorded in a holy book? Holding to this highly Eurocentric concept, we could say that civilisations are historically shifting cultural and identity complexes, defining themselves only in dialectical and syncretic interaction with neighbouring cultures.[6]

We should therefore replace the philosophical observation of human incompleteness with the idea of the plasticity of the human being,

---

[6] See Kilani in Galissot, Kilani, Rivera, 2000: 9-31.

both as an individual and as a species. The plasticity of the human being, both in terms of its organism and its mental faculties, stems from its particularly well-developed genetic and, above all, neuronal orientation towards virtuality. This plasticity in relation to virtuality requires a constant cultural construction of the human being, in its individual and collective identity, and in relation to a particular milieu. It is a complex process of construction, both creative and communal, involving artisanal and technical practices reminiscent of the Promethean arts, as well as the semiotic (Prometheus again) and aesthetic processes of symbolic expression and realisation.

From the contemporary perspective offered by the field of genetics, the most advanced and critical practitioners of the life sciences have made it abundantly clear that the development of the human genome cannot be viewed exclusively by analogy with coded phrases that can be deciphered deterministically. The "transcription" of DNA into "messenger" RNA, resulting in its "translation" into the amino acid sequences that sustain and control the cells that make up our living organism, cannot be understood in isolation from its epigenetic and physiological environment on the one hand, and its interaction with its biophysical environment on the other. Here again we are faced with a network of complex relations of continuity, porosity, and reciprocity, which is beyond any model of linear logic or purely causal determinism.[7] Genetic processes must be envisaged within a multi-deterministic framework marked by a degree of randomness; in this sense, genetics and biotechnologies should be considered as human sciences, of a hermeneutic order. As is the case with even the most sophisticated "scientific" medical research, the life sciences are humans knowledge of the human. The material, psychic, technical, social, and cultural environment plays a decisive interactive role both in the development of this knowledge and in the processes it identifies.

Almost forty years ago, a neurobiologist, a geneticist, and a psychologist jointly asserted the absence of any determinism,

[7] References in Calame, 2010: 60-87 and 172-283.

whether biological or cultural, in human development. Criticising a linear and mechanistic determinism that originated in bourgeois ideology, the three scientists demonstrated the "interpenetration" that exists between the (human) organism and its environment. They argued that there are no general rules that could describe how different genotypes develop differently in different environments:

Organisms do not simply adapt to previously existing, autonomous environments; they create, destroy, modify, and internally transform aspects of the external world by their own life activities to make this environment. Just as there is no organism without an environment, so there is no environment without an organism.[8]

In its extreme diversification, this complex and interactive process of cultural and social construction of the human, both in and through relations with their peers and with their environment, can be conceived in operational terms of "anthropopoiesis" and "ecopoiesis": anthropopoiesis as the physical and psychic construction of the human in social, political, cultural, and even religious interaction with others, which is then combined with ecopoiesis as the indispensable constructive and cultural interaction with an environment.[9] The concept of the anthropopoietic and ecopoietic identity of a human being who constructs themselves as a human being in their indispensable interdependence with an environmental and social milieu makes it possible to overcome the nature/culture dualism.

Indeed, the idea of the organic, ecological, social, and cultural construction of the human being in interaction with a milieu invites us to approach both the human constitution and humans' environment in terms of porosity and plasticity, as conceived in particular by the neuronal sciences. Because of the plasticity and permeability that characterise the human being, particularly in its neuronal and intellectual constitution, humans' genetic dispositions, organic-neuronal capacities, and physical-psychic and intellectual

---

[8] Rose, Lewontin, Kamin, 1984: 265-290; p. 273 for the citation.

[9] On the possible critical uses of the operative concept of anthropo-poiesis, see in particular Remotti's proposals in Affergan et al. 2003: 17-74; see also Remotti, 2013: 4-19 and 33-59 (= 1999, in the first version of this work in French translation).

faculties can only be realised in relation to and in interaction with a particular biophysical environment and social and cultural milieu; the exercise of these capacities contributes to a reciprocal shaping and configuring of both human and milieu. This system of feedback is constantly overlooked in the contemporary neoliberal paradigm that sees the individual as being called upon to realise themselves in an egocentric performance, in competition with others, for their own profit.

From the point of view of the cultural construction of the human on the basis of, on the one hand, certain biological and neuronal factors, and, on the other hand, an ecological, social, and cultural environment, gender identities and relations take on particular significance, together with the representations that are made of them in different cultures. This is borne out by the anthropological and comparative study of gendered identities and social relations. The physical markers of the differentiated biological and procreative functions of women and men are transformed into institutional and social relations; sexual organs and secondary sexual characteristics, to use the concept developed by Sigmund Freud, are then the basis of practices and representations that vary greatly from one culture to another. In different ecologies, these representations are the foundation of social and symbolic relations, which are, unfortunately, generally hierarchically structured... Thus, having been integrated into symbolic representations that make extensive use of metaphor, or which are even systematically manipulated, differences in biological sex are "culturalised" according to the ecological and social context where they develop.[10]

The anthropopoietic and ecopoietic perspective on the social and cultural construction of men and women in interaction with a milieu thus allows us to comprehensively address the question of the complex relationship between the innate and the acquired. As far as we are concerned, the innate part is of a biological, genetic, and

---

[10] On this subject, see the work of Françoise Héritier, writing from a perspective that is still very much influenced by structural anthropology; for example, Héritier, 1996: 205-235.

neuronal order; but this innate constitution can only develop its potentialities, on the basis of a specific body, in a biophysical ecology and a social and cultural environment on which the human being, integrated in a community, acts reciprocally.

IV

THE HUMAN BEING AND ITS ENVIRONMENT: INTERACTIVE RELATIONSHIPS

The necessary and constitutive character of the interaction between the human being and its environment therefore requires a shift from a philosophical conception to an anthropopoietic and ecopoietic, and therefore globally anthropological understanding of the human being. Such a perspective on the human and its milieu undoubtedly requires both the abandonment of the structuralist split between nature and culture, both of which have become universalised and reified concepts, and the elaboration of a new conception of the environment of the human being living in a community.

1. *Umgebung* and *Umwelt?* (Natural) Environment and Milieu?

To that end, might it be useful to draw on the distinction proposed by the biologist and philosopher Jakob von Uexküll regarding the milieu? In relation to human (and also animal) perception and action, he distinguishes *Umgebung*, the environment as an "objective given", from *Umwelt*, the environment as an "ambient world". More precisely, according to von Uexküll, the distinction to be made is between *Umgebung* as the external world, *Umwelt* as a singular perception (in space and time) of the environment, and *Innenwelt* as the internal world that is constituted through *Umwelt*.[1]

Augustin Berque, however, reduces this to a binary opposition, and opportunely reminds us that this distinction partly overlaps with that which was made by the Japanese philosopher Watsuji Tetsuro:[2] on the one hand, *shizen kankyô* as a natural environment, an environmental given; on the other hand, *fûdo* as a human milieu, a localised natural and historical complex, a set of natural and cultural

[1] Von Uexküll, 1921: 3-12.

[2] Berque, 2010: 199-208.

features in a given region. Watsuji Tetsuro adds a spatial dimension to the meaning of this second term by adding the suffix -*sei*, which indicates the idea of locality: he thus proposes the concept of *fûdosei*, as a structural moment of human existence, a "regionality". The French philosopher and geographer pursues this idea using the concepts of "médiance" and "trajection" between subject and object; at the level of the individual, this concept of "médiance" essentially corresponds to the definition of a (human) culture for a subject situated opposite an objectified nature.[3]

But is it possible for humans to perceive an environment that is "natural", that is entirely external to them, that is objectified as nature? Both from the point of view of the classical theory of knowledge and aesthetics and from the perspective of the neural sciences, perception through the intermediary of one's own body involves the creation of a representation of the object. Organic perception involves the sensory and intellectual, if not cognitive, construction of a reality that we objectify as external in order to better act upon it. Ludwig Wittgenstein thus distinguishes between *Vorstellung* and *Darstellung* in order to better define, alongside conceptual representation of a cognitive nature, the mode of "presentation" (*darstellen*), which amounts to figuring (*abbilden*) and showing: "What a picture represents is its sense" ("*Was das Bild darstellt ist sein Sinn*").[4]

However, the procedures of "presentation" and showing depend on our sensory apparatus; before any conceptual knowledge can arise by means of schematisation, categorisation, and abstract modelling, those procedures produce a representation of the object in order to make it communicable, to share it. And sensory interaction is accompanied by practical interaction. Through cultural, anthropopoietic, and ecopoietic practices, which vary from one community to another and from one milieu to another, human

---

[3] See also Berque, 2014: 89-119 (= 2019 in English translation), and forthcoming.

[4] Wittgenstein, 2021: § 2.221; see also § 2.201: "A picture depicts reality [*das Bild bildet die Wirklichkeit ab*] by representing [*darstellt*] a possibility of existence and non-existence of states of affairs [*Sachverhalte*]"; cf. Borutti, 2006: 4 and 39.

beings draw from their environment the resources that, firstly, ensure their material survival, and secondly, support their symbolic development in society, as cultural beings. In these two ways, humans interactively modify their animal, vegetal, and physical environment, and their survival and identity as human beings, social and cultural beings, depends on this biochemical continuity.

Here, then, we perhaps find "*médiance*", and even "*trajection*", as proposed by Berque, but neither between a subject and an object, nor between an objective *Umgebung* and an *Umwelt* experienced by an individual or a collective group through a logical operation of predication between the former and the latter. As Georges Canguilhem remarks, who also takes up Uexküll's concept of *Umwelt* as a behavioural milieu specific to a given organism:

> *From the biological point of view, one must understand that the relationship between the organism and the environment is the same as that between the parts and the whole of an organism. The individuality of the living does not stop at its ectodermic borders any more than it begins at the cell. [...]. The milieu of behavior proper to the living* (Umwelt) *is an ensemble of excitations, which have the value and signification of signals.*[5]

Because of the necessary and constitutive interaction between humans and their environment, the *Umgebung* can only be *Umwelt*, the environment can only be milieu; and, just as for the humans civilised by Aeschylus's Prometheus, it is a meaningful *Umwelt*. We can include in this interaction with the environment-milieu the understanding that we have now acquired of it in terms of physics and, especially, biology.

Thanks to our earlier detour through Greco-Roman antiquity, which allows us to cast a critical eye on modernity, we can now make use of Prometheus, semiotic systems, and *tékhnai*. Without interaction with its environment, the human being is only an ant who looks without seeing and listens without hearing – so says Prometheus, as

---

[5] Canguilhem, 1952/2008: 111.

presented by Aeschylus to the Athenian public of the fifth century BC. Only the technical arts, which are dependent on humans' own practical intelligence, enable them to activate their sensory capacities, to decipher in the environment the features that will make it into a signifying whole, and to draw from this "semiotised" environment the resources necessary for supporting life and the means of coping, to a certain extent, with the hazards and finiteness of the mortal condition. All of this is practised by humans without exceeding the limits assigned to them at the moment of their separation from the world of the gods: the possible *húbris* in the use of the *tékhnai* invented and granted to man by Prometheus remind us of the *húbris* also inscribed, in another form, in the hero's destiny!

But from the Greek (and Promethean) regime of a cosmic *phúsis* that, through the interpretative work of mortals, becomes endowed with meaning and thus orientates humans' practices towards it, let us move on to the contemporary scientific paradigm. For example, this paradigm, envisaging a "nature" composed of complex living organisms, involves the mechanistic deciphering of the genome and the technological application of genetic engineering, as mentioned in the previous chapter. Does this mean that, henceforth, it is no longer nature, but the vegetal, animal, and human genome that has become a semiotic system, lending itself to technical interventions by humans? Has the "book of life" replaced both the "book of nature" and the "book of culture"?

2. Interpretative Technical Arts Confiscated by Capitalism

Our decentred and critical view of (post-)modernity, which is made possible by our anthropological approach to the culture of Classical Athens, has led us to a negative response to the matter at hand: as I mentioned above, and have discussed elsewhere,[6] the deterministic model underlying genetics, that of a coded message to be deciphered in a unilinear way, does not take into account epigenetic factors, nor the countless parameters implicated in the material and cultural

---

[6] Calame, 2010: 131-140.

environment that is indispensable for the (phylo- and onto-) genetic development of the human being. The genetic part of the human being should be understood in the context of an interactional and contextualised multi-determinism, marked by a degree of randomness.[7] We have seen that the technical arts granted to humans by Prometheus, according to Aeschylus's play, which include agriculture, trade, writing, medicine, and divination, correspond to practices that are notably based on the perception and reading of signs in the environment. They are therefore interpretative arts, as is the modern field of genetics: this human science par excellence – both in its knowledge and practice – involves the reading of gene sequences and the identification of the part they play, in complex combination with other processes, in the biological development of the organism, and especially the human organism.

It is therefore evident that, to varying degrees and at different times, profound changes to the environment are brought about by humans' sensory and intelligent apprehension of their *Umwelt*, they are brought about by their perception of and practices towards an environment that is indispensable to their survival in society, and by the cultural dimension of practices towards a world that is subject to technical arts of a hermeneutic nature. While is it true that the environment shapes human beings, who cannot survive without the material, social, and cultural determinations that shape their identity, at the same time the intelligent and practical actions of human communities contribute to shaping and modifying that environment. The indispensable interaction between humans and their environment has a multiple historicity; it is limited by the finiteness of a world that has limits of its own.

With regard to this necessary interaction between human beings and their various milieux, the practical and technical developments that have been driven by the European boom in the "natural" sciences

---

[7] See also, for example, Testart, Sinaï, Bourgain, 2010: 53-62, regarding the "new construction of the human body". The same is undoubtedly true of the new technological fantasies fostered by the project for an "augmented human", particularly through the application of artificial intelligence; see, for example, the various contributions to the volume edited by Boyer-Bévière and Moine-Dupuis, 2020.

since the eighteenth century have had a decisive impact on the environment, the scale of which we are starting to understand: the impoverishment of the soil, the pollution of water and the depletion of aquifers, the consequences of disorderly and destructive urbanisation, the results of the exploitation of non-renewable energy resources, and finally the critical impact on the climate resulting from various forms of soil pollution and, above all, atmospheric pollution. The objectification of a nature viewed as something to be dominated by human reason and its technical practices for utilitarian purposes led to an industrialisation whose undeniable benefits, in terms of material and social utility, were swiftly appropriated.

Indeed, the benefits of industrialisation were rapidly submitted to the logic of the capitalist economy. Motivated by the consumerist productivism that follows from it, driven by the imperative of growth measured in purely economic and financial terms, and more recently intensified by the neoliberal ideology, the objectification of nature in opposition to human culture has led to both these elements being thought of in terms of "resources": natural and human resources to be exploited with a view to economic return and financial profit for the benefit of the richest countries and those with the most technologically developed military strength. This imperative for productivity, framed in the purely financial terms of profit maximisation and a globalisation that amounts to a new form of colonialism, is largely based on the rapid development of increasingly sophisticated technologies. While information and communication technologies have undoubtedly contributed to the growth and rapidity of the almost universal circulation of knowledge and experience, they have also brought about the digitisation and virtualisation of social connections and exchanges between people, as well as making it more difficult to process information in an interpretative and practical way.

It is now well known that the terrestrial and climatic environment, along with human communities, is suffering the increasingly destructive consequences of an entirely anthropocentric economic anthropology, inspired by Anglo-American (economic) liberalism. This anthropology is in fact based on the sole motivation of individual (financial) profit and capitalist accumulation, with an emphasis on commodification, efficiency, competitiveness, and productivity. The keywords of the neoliberal newspeak are "liberalisation" (the deregulation of both economic exchange and the financial sector, to the benefit of the rich), "reform" (always in the sense of the progressive and systematic dismantling of public services in the fields of health, education, pensions, transport, and communications), "private ownership" (aimed at privatising profits and nationalising losses, especially in the banking sector), "globalisation" (to allow neocolonial and patriarchal investment practices by multinationals in low-income countries, with a view to exploiting their raw materials and "human resources"), and finally "the market" (designating a market economy elevated to a dogma that reflects the basic functioning of capitalism).[8] This "rhetoric of capitalist fetishism" has not been curbed in any way by the 2008 banking crisis, not by the Covid-19 pandemic.[9] The principle of (free and undistorted) competition based on a methodological individualism, with a focus on the development of the individual in the singularity of their "self" and the satisfaction of their personal interests, is by definition opposed to the principle of constructive interaction between individuals, human communities, and their milieux.

In spite of the prospect of economic and financial profits that they seem to offer, it is paradoxically the life sciences that may be capable of reversing the trend. Like genetics, which we have likened to the Promethean technical arts, the life sciences demonstrate that it is the milieu (internal and external) that shapes the human, both in terms of the body and individual identity; in response, the field of cultural

---

[8] See Bihr, 2007.

[9] The different stages of the hegemonic establishment of the neoliberal model through capitalist globalisation are well outlined in particular by Massiah, 2011: 14-54; for an analysis of the foundations of the financial crisis of 2007-2008, see Millet & Toussaint, 2010: 41-63. For the implications of the economic, social and environmental crisis triggered by the coronavirus epidemic, the "first crisis of the Anthropocene", see the good pages of Tanuro, 2020: 17-39.

anthropology is attempting to understand this complex shaping process in terms of interaction, based on a conception of exceptional biological and neuronal plasticity. From an anthropopoietic and ecopoietic anthropological perspective, I would add that the necessary shaping of humans, in their biological and neuronal individuality, by their material and social environment allows them, in return, to act on this same environment. This double movement undoubtedly entails a new, non-Kantian theory of knowledge: to know oneself is to know one's physical and cultural environment; and to know what appears to us as the external world is to modify it while modifying ourselves (there are no pre-existing structures of perception). This is the logical consequence of the human being's biological and neuronal sensitivity and plasticity in relation to the physical, biochemical, social, and cultural environment that sustains its existence. And the practical consequence is that this environment is itself constantly being reshaped by the practices of humans, depending on their perceptions, knowledge, and representations of that environment.

What is more, this means that even the most formal and "hard" sciences, those that use the most sophisticated mathematical models and, like the field of genetics, benefit from the most sophisticated tools of information processing and computer modelling, are also effectively arts and knowledge of an interpretative order. In fact, it is for this very reason that the practices and applications issuing from these sciences can be geared towards a neoliberal anthropology and capitalist processes of appropriation: they transform them into sources of financial profit, without regard for any social and cultural utility.

V

FOR AN ECOSOCIALIST UNDERSTANDING OF HUMANS AND THEIR MILIEU

What lies, then, "beyond nature and culture"? Animism, totemism, analogism, or naturalism: these are the four paradigms of being-in-the-world for humans, the four "ontologies" that can define the relationship between human beings and their environment, according to the analysis of Philippe Descola in his foundational work *Par-delà nature et culture* ("*Beyond Nature and Culture*") (2005). Faced with our urgent need, both ideological and political, to leave behind the dichotomy between nature and culture, does the process of contemporary ecopoietic anthropopoiesis allow us to move beyond these four "'ontological" paradigms and find a fifth possibility?

These four paradigms are, in the definition given by Descola, as many "models" regulating the relations of humans, as cultural beings, with a nature that is defined from the outset as an environment made up of "non-humans". They would therefore correspond to four cosmologies, in which humans' complex relations with their environment can be considered in terms of structural transformations. Whereas animism tends to project human interiority onto the diversity of the surrounding world, naturalism connects the diverse cultural expressions of humans to the universal laws of the physical and biological world; in other words, in the first paradigm the human subject projects an "interiority" similar to their own onto a different "physicality", and in the second paradigm humans constitute external entities as objects that lack interiority, but present a physicality similar to their own. On the other hand, whereas totemism corresponds to a system of reciprocal equivalences between physicalities and interiorities, analogism tends to fragment everything that exists into discrete entities, which are both different but also similar to one another, then to integrate them into a system in which they become intelligible by means of the resemblances that are the basis of the analogical process; thus, in totemic ontology, the object shares traits of interiority and physicality with humans while maintaining certain differences, whereas, for the ontology of analogism, the interiority and physicality of the object are distinguished from those of the subject, while allowing for the establishment of relations of correspondence.

Surely the devastation that sustains our lives, and especially the climate emergency, invite us to abandon our adherence to a deeply ingrained naturalism? Surely it is now time to imagine, in the context of globalised capitalist neoliberalism and its destructive effects on human communities and their milieux, a fifth paradigm capable of rebalancing the relationship between those communities and their milieux?

1. The Anthropocene: Towards a New Naturalism?

One might object that, by adopting Descola's distinction between, on the one hand, an interiority corresponding to a consciousness made up of intentionality, subjectivity, reflexivity, affects, and imagination, and, on the other hand, a physicality that includes material substance and physiological, perceptive, and sensorimotor processes (but also ways of acting), we are at risk of restoring the split between culture and nature. And the risk seems all the greater if we project this distinction onto entities external to humans. Through the intermediary of ontologies whose status (mental, cultural?) has yet to be defined, we are implicitly drawing a distinction between interior and exterior, or even between the spiritual and the material; we are undoubtedly also drawing a distinction between the human and the non-human.

This last point is contested by Jean-Marie Schaeffer, a specialist in aesthetics, who maintains the radical position that the thesis of the "human exception" must be refuted by an uncompromising naturalism. In his view, in a reversal of the usual anthropocentric theses, humanity itself must be considered first as a biological form of life; it is the biological specificity of humans that allows them to constitute themselves as social (and cultural) beings. Fundamentally, the human social fact is a biological fact, and therefore "the biology of the human is constitutively social".[1]

In any case, for both the anthropologist Descola and the philosopher Schaeffer, whether it is a question of ontologies that configure our relations with non-humans or whether it is necessary to adopt a principled naturalism, the distinction between nature and culture is now obsolete. From the perspective of the naturalism promulgated by the latter, culture is a fact of nature, and is therefore "part of the biological identity of the human species". The specificity of the human cannot be understood in terms of an opposition between nature and culture since "every species transforms its environment at the same time as it is transformed by it. Culture should simply be considered as one of the processes that brings about such a transformation".[2] Descola, meanwhile, recognises that there is always a symbolic and practical interaction with what we have isolated as "nature" with a view to exploiting it for our own benefit. Their shared judgement of the particular naturalism inherent to the contemporary Western paradigm is clear: the Cartesian idea of the possibility of man's domination over a nature of which he is the owner has brought about the pollution and destructive climatic effects of which we have finally become aware.[3]

This brings us back to the question of the practical impact of the ideological division between nature and culture. In this respect, the notion of humans' entry into the "Anthropocene" era could contribute to the conception of a fifth mode of humans' interaction with their environment. Whether one situates the start of this era at the moment of the beginning of agriculture in the Near East 11,000

---

[1] Schaeffer, 2007: 201-269. See also the critical remarks made by the same Schaeffer, 2007: 29-35, in relation to the principle of the four ontologies described by Descola (2005).

[2] Schaeffer, 2007: 224 and 226.

[3] Descola, 2010: 33-39.

years ago, the development of European colonialism from 1492 onwards, the arrival of the Industrial Revolution, the nuclear age, or the "great acceleration" of the 1950s, the Anthropocene is posited as a "new geological age of the Earth", succeeding that of the Holocene.[4] In terms of the "terrestrial ecosystem", this geological periodisation is based on the impact of the development of human communities and their technical arts on the biosphere and, in particular, on the climate.

Four narratives have arisen concerning the consequences of the Anthropocene, each with their own interpretation of our relationship with our environment, and the geological transformation that has been brought about by the thermo-industrial revolution.

According to the first of these narratives, responsibility for controlling human actions in relation to nature should be entrusted to those who have brought about the consequences for the "Earth system" of growth based on technical innovation: in other words, scientists. A second understanding of the Anthropocene calls into question the established division between nature and culture that underpins Western modernity; it entails a new philosophical conception of human freedom in the context of the finiteness of the planet, in a "Promethean" perspective that envisages a new form of planetary management by means of geo-engineering, based on techno-scientific solutions that do not challenge financial capitalism. A third narrative of our entry into the Anthropocene leads, conversely, to a rejection of techno-scientific solutions as a way of addressing global ecological and climatic disturbances; it leads instead to the defence of a process of "degrowth", involving modes of production and consumption marked by sobriety and an emancipatory concept of wellbeing. Finally, an "eco-Marxist reading" of the Anthropocene provides a narrative emphasising the effects of capitalism and its globalised mode of production on the

---

[4] See Bonneuil & Fressot, 2016: 28-32, who resolutely and conclusively associate the beginning of the Anthropocene with the start of the Industrial Revolution. The "great acceleration" thesis is defended in particular by Lewis & Maslin, 2015.

world-system, both in terms of the human and social dimension and with regard to nature, which is now being assessed for its economic value in order to subject it to the "rules" of the market.[5]

Whatever the overlaps and points of difference between these four "narratives", one feature that they all share is their consistently anthropocentric perspective: the human is viewed as acting on an earth, which (like the Anthropocene itself!) is endowed with a capital letter to indicate that it is a unified whole: humans' environment thus becomes the "Earth system", or is assimilated to a "Nature" with which humans should enter into a contract on an equal footing, or alternatively the ecosystem is theorised as a living organism governed by the regulating principle of homeostasis.

This new form of ontologisation of nature, henceforth understood as an Earth system, has been extensively developed in the form of the anthropomorphic figure of Gaia, notably adopted by James Lovelock. This anthropomorphisation of the earth in the image of a human organism once again effectively posits a nature that, even though it is instituted as a biosphere, is separate from certain beings who are an integral part of it: humans in their social and cultural communities. In light of this separation, it is fruitless to try to restore, under the misleading name of Gaia, a nature vaguely defined (in Latour's words) as "the localised, historical, and profane avatars of Nature" (endowed with a capital letter…); a Nature from which Humans sought to emancipate themselves while, having become Terrestrials, they remained attached to a Gaia (treated grammatically as a plural by Latour), as "new political entities", in accordance with a "New Climate Regime"…[6] It is equally fruitless to propose a post-environmental neo-Promethean perspective that attributes to

---

[5] These four narratives are described by Bonneuil & Fressoz, https://blogs.mediapart.fr/edition/les-possibles/article/230514/lanthropocene-et-ses-lectures-politiques; that article summarises the theses developed in their book of 2016: 223-279. See also the chapter by Sinaï, 2013, who argues that the consequences of our entry into the Anthropocene oblige us to pursue "degrowth": on this concept, open to dispute, see the references given chap. V n. 31. On the "intrisic economic value" attributed to nature, see chap. V note 35.

[6] The citations are taken from the sophistic propositions formulated by Latour, 2015a, 355-368 (p. 358 for the quotation); for a critical discussion of these ideas, see Calame, 2020-21.

humans, situated in relation to a new techno-nature, the power to take on a genuine "planetary governance"; this "governance" is supposed to involve a system of production that would be transformed into a "system of engendering", supported by a "new ecological class" capable of fighting against a generalised "economisation" through the reappropriation of "le politique" (!). All that new process is envisaged as taking place in the context of a "united Europe", in the name of a "higher rationality"…[7]

Let us mention in passing that several ecofeminist movements, both essentialist and fundamentalist in their approach, have attempted to revive the Hellenic figure of Gaia: as an inspirational and founding figure, Gaia is then used to embody, in opposition to the patriarchal power exercised by humans over nature, an Earth that is not only personified but also divinised.

This rereading and re-creation of Greek myths leads in particular to a representation of Gaia as "the ancient Earth-Mother who brought forth the world and the human race from 'the gaping void, Chaos'". The primordial and totemic figure of Gaia is portrayed as inviting us to take action in the present, and through the active revival of the (recreated) Hellenic myth, the modern woman, subjected to patriarchal socialisation, is called upon to experience an ontological revolution. Through this evocation of a "thealogical" order, she is invited to immerse herself in a sacred space, in contact with different manifestations of the Goddess, a Mother Earth associated with the fertility of the fields and of the womb…[8]

From a less theological perspective, we should also mention the work and ecofeminist commitments of the Indian physicist Vandana Shiva, who has become well known for her tireless advocacy for organic farming based on traditional agricultural practices, for the rejection of large-scale agriculture requiring fertilisers, pesticides,

---

[7] This refers, once again, to the vague and misleading concepts put forward by Latour, 2015b: 154, and 2017: 113-115, as well as Latour and Schultz, 2022: 82-85. This approach notably avoids any condemnation of capitalism and the neoliberal ideology that supports it.

[8] Spretnak, 1992: XIII-XIV.

GMOs, and patents on seeds, and for biodiversity in general, against the agri-food practices imposed by multinational companies for the benefit of the richest countries based on a logic of patriarchal domination. At the end of one of her essays, she expresses her respect for an "Earth", spelt with a capital letter and associated with the feminine, but not identified with any particular divinity; and in her preface to the second edition of Ariel Salleh's *Ecofeminsim as Politics*, she states that the anthropocentric reasoning of capitalism denies "the creativity of nature, and hence Rights of Mother Earth".[9]

Passing from Brahmanic culture to the indigenous cultures of Central America, we also encounter the figure of Pachamama, the Mother Earth figure who inhabits and sustains the cosmogony of the Aymaras and Quechuas, the Amerindian peoples of the Andes. She is the object of regular offerings and supports the fertility of the land and the resulting abundance of agricultural resources. She is identified with Nature, and provided some of the inspiration for the granting of rights to the Earth, which was successively enshrined in the constitution of Ecuador in 2008 and in the constitution of Bolivia in 2010. Article 71 of the Ecuadorian constitution now states that: "Nature, or Pacha Mama, where life is produced and reproduced, has the right to be fully respected with regard to its existence and the maintenance and regeneration of vital cycles, its structure, its functions, and its evolutionary processes. Any person, community, village, or nationality can demand that the public authority respect the rights of nature".[10] Once again, through theological (if not thealogical) means, nature is essentialised (if not made sacred), before becoming a subject of law. However, whether it is considered as a divine entity or not, one might wonder how the earth will be able to stand before any court of justice and asserts its rights in an autonomous way...

---

[9] Shiva, 1988: 215-227; cf. Burgart Goutal, 2020: 91-92 and 272-284.

[10] See the references given in this regard by Solón, 2017. For objections to constituting "nature" as a person and a subject of law, see Calame, 2020-21.

2. The "Ecopoiesis" Paradigm for Women and Men

Wherever we place the beginning of this process, it is now clear that our societies, dominated by industrialisation and technologies, along with the financial profits that can be derived from them, have entered a new period that is referred to, rightly or wrongly, as the Anthropocene, or even the Capitalocene; the practical and technical interaction of humans with their environment is now so extensive that it is endangering the milieu that is indispensable for life for every human community. However, aside from any ontology – whether anthropological or not – and aside from any classification of geological ages, I propose to use the concept of "ecopoiesis" to describe this new paradigm. Indeed, in addition to the impact on the environment and, ultimately, on the climate of the mechanistic techniques and technologies that have enabled industrialisation, we must also consider processes such as the genetic manipulation of organisms facilitated by the life sciences. These manipulations concern plants and animals as well as humans; they affect both humans and their milieu, and, more globally, the biosphere, while, in the capitalist regime, multinational pharmaceutical and agri-food industries derive enormous profits from those processes.

However, we must move from this techno-capitalist "ecopoiesis" to a concept of "anthropopoietic ecopoiesis", not for reasons of Hellenistic erudition but so as to integrate the social and cultural dimension of the interaction between humans and their milieu.[11] "Anthropopoietic ecopoiesis" refers to the not only technical, but also social and cultural construction of the human in relation to its environment and in interaction with it. The concept is intended both to avoid the new form of naturalism, or even behaviourism, that is

---

[11] The concept of "ecopoiesis" is also a tribute to the work of Augustin Berque, who defines the "ecumene" as "the ecological, technical, and symbolic relationship of humanity to the expanse of the earth" (2010: 17); however, by pure coincidence it is also found in the title of the journal *Ecopoiesis: Eco-Human Theory and Practice*, founded in Russia in 2020, whose aim is to offer "a vibrant forum of theories and practices aimed at harmonizing the relations of mankind and the natural world in the interests of sustainable development, the creation of Eco-Humanity as a new community of human beings and more-than-human world"; the journal endeavours to show that human beings are "ecological" beings who are not separate from the world, and who, as such, bear "an aesthetic responsibility to the fate of the earth, to transform devastation into beauty". https://en.ecopoiesis.ru/manifesto.

often produced by the cognitive sciences, and to adopt an explicit attitude of anthropological and political criticism in relation to our current mode of existence in what is identified as the Anthropocene, if not the Capitalocene.

In an age marked by the prevalence of "ecopoiesis", the life sciences and the neural sciences are showing the constitutive permeability of orders that were previously considered distinct – the physical, the vegetal, the animal, and the human – for better or for worse. Across the fields of physics, chemistry, biology, and the human sciences, these orders are now integrated into an extremely complex interactive system: a complex system that is not so much a product of complex thought, but rather a product of a way of thinking about complexity. This is a way of thinking that is capable of taking into account systems that, like non-linear dynamic systems, are interconnected at different levels of organisation; they include phenomena of self-organisation, emergence, bifurcations, multiple causalities (linear or circular), non-linear interactions, noise or chaos phenomena, etc.[12]

The representatives of the life sciences now recognise this state of affairs: not only are the biological or neuronal processes they have identified, such as the development of cells or the functioning of synapses, subject to a multi-determinism that is not necessarily linear; but cellular developments and neuronal processes also depend on complex interactions both with the organic environment and with the social and cultural context of their actualisation; and this is without taking into account the element of randomness which, as in the case of genetics, marks their deployment. Thus, at the turn of the twentieth century, in contrast to the destructive impact on the environment and the climate of the mechanistic technologies that, as we have said, enabled industrialisation subject to capitalist productivism and the market (or alternatively subject to Soviet-style centralised planning and productivism), the decisive advances of the life sciences and the neural sciences also appeared. Both of these

---

[12] For a recent formulation of these ideas, see Guespin-Michel, 2015: 18-29 and 46-59.

have fundamentally called into question the relationship of humans, with their social and cultural practices, with a nature wrongly objectified as a set of resources to be exploited.

However, as the life sciences are now developing mainly in the context of the Anglo-American neoliberal regime, they are particularly solicited with a view to the financial profit that can be extracted from their various developments and applications. This is the case, for example, with the genetic manipulation of living organisms, whether this concerns plants, animals, or humans. These practices depend on biological and biotechnological knowledge which is largely exploited and monopolised by the commercial logic of certain large multinationals that, in the agro-chemical and pharmaco-medical fields, control a purely economic globalisation through the use of patents. Under the pretext of making a generous and progressive contribution to the food and health of the human race, such companies implicitly share Descartes's conception of the domination of nature by humans! The hegemonic spread of GMOs and the launch of numerous gene therapies are thus contributing to a new productivism. Indeed, as potential *ophelémata* in the Promethean sense of technical practices offering an advantage to humans, gene technologies applied to plants or humans are monopolised by agri-food and pharmaceutical transnationals, under the control of the sacrosanct patents that protect "intellectual property".[13] In this way, these conglomerates, specialists in "tax optimisation", maintain a monopoly, while restricting both organic agriculture centred on basic food crops and the spread of low-cost generic products for treating endemic and epidemic diseases. We should recall here that it took more than two years for the pharmaceutical companies involved to grant a very limited waiver of the intellectual property concerning vaccines against Covid-19…

Thus, in their use of technosciences, the large agri-food and chemical groups are taking possession of discoveries, transformed into inventions, while stripping them of the principle of civil utility that

---

[13] See the examples given in the book published by ATTAC, 2012: 54-56.

was central to the Promethean (and also Cartesian) concept of technical arts. Powerful transnational companies such as Monsanto or Syngenta, in the fields of agri-food and agrochemicals, are removing from biotechnologies their possible social utility in order to submit them exclusively to the demands of capitalist profit and monopolies. Aside from their possible negative effects on human health and soil quality, the spread of GMOs contributes, for example, to the impoverishment of small farmers who are forced to go into debt each year to buy new seeds and are led to abandon local food crops.[14] Meanwhile, in the domain of health, the monopolistic policies of the international pharmaceutical companies are devoted to the development of sophisticated therapies, such as gene therapies; yet, whatever the effectiveness of such gene therapies (which is disputed), their high cost means that they are restricted to a wealthy minority of the population of the richest countries, to the detriment of research into some diseases that affect vast numbers of people. In 2011, for example, the WHO identified fourteen tropical diseases that affect one billion people in the world's poorest countries, but which do not attract significant levels of investment from pharmaceutical and biotechnology transnationals.[15]

It has also been shown that the paradigm shift associated with the new form of individualism characteristic of the neoliberal economy has led to the failure of the medical project of setting up banks (*sic*) of genetic data. The clinical use of the DNA sequences collected in national biobanks, driven by the hope of making substantial profits, has proved to be unreliable, to say the least, partly because several genes may be involved in the onset of a disease, partly because of the epigenetic factors mentioned above, and partly because of the influence of individual contexts.[16] And new neurotechnologies seem to be confronted with the same difficulties in terms of ensuring that their use is safe for humans and socially sustainable. We should be

---

[14] See the essay published by ATTAC, 2005.

[15] http://www.who.int/topics/tropical_diseases/factsheets/neglected/fr/. See also some figures on this from Testart, Sinai, Bourgain, 2010: 102-104.

[16] Rose & Rose, 2012: 158-216.

particularly wary of the promises of economic efficiency made by actors in the fields of bioeconomy and neuroeconomy, based on basic behaviourism and a logic of financial gain...[17]

The concept of anthropopoietic ecopoiesis therefore allows us not only to avoid ontologies and designations of a geological nature, but also, and especially, to call out the illusions of so-called "sustainable development" or the "green economy": these are nothing more than the ecological alibis – the "greenwash" – of a way of thinking that is attached to productivist growth, centred on increasing GDP, and the principles of competition and competitiveness (in a race to the bottom with regard to wages and taxation). By claiming to establish property rights over the resources of "nature", by appropriating the major ecological functions of the planet and subjecting them to a system of exchange value, the green economy merely constitutes the biosphere as a vast private enterprise. Thus, by constituting nature as a stock of resources and drawing on various entrepreneurial strategies, the neoliberal advocates of the green economy intend to subject the earth itself to financial investment and the "laws" of the market, and consequently to capitalist profit.[18] Their credo of "green growth" turns out to be a pure "mirage".[19]

Once again, through a process of generalised commodification, we find the domination of the planet and the biosphere, for economic and financial profit, by a tiny minority of financially powerful individuals, and to the advantage of transnational companies owned by super-rich oligarchs. In contrast, we therefore propose an anthropopoietic "ecopoiesis", involving the construction of men and women alike in an emancipated culture of solidarity, and an interactive construction in relation to their biological and social living milieu. This "ecopoiesis", both political and social in nature, is an

---

[17] See the excellent chapter on this subject in Azam, 2015: 165-209.

[18] ATTAC, 2012: 79-126; see also the critique of green capitalism by Tanuro, 2020: 93-123.

[19] I am here paraphrasing the title of the chapter that Kempf, 2009: 75-108, devotes to the modes of energy production and consumption involved in globalised capitalism in order to show that "the technological choice is essentially a political choice that derives from a prior conception of social organisation" (p. 108).

ecosocialist "ecopoiesis" aimed at addressing the inevitable and necessary, but highly complex interaction between humans and their environment, between human communities and their milieux, between the basic material and social needs of humans and the means of balanced satisfaction provided by their environment.

Indeed, the ecological and ecopoietic imperative is not only of an epistemological order, but also economic and, ultimately, political. Faced with the productivism imposed by the capitalist economy and the generalised commodification of relations of production and social and human relations, but also faced with the pretensions of a sustainable or green economy that remains fundamentally attached to the principles of the market as the ultimate regulating authority, the only viable option is a radical break.[20] In this ecosocialist transformation, the relations of production and the productive apparatus themselves would be rethought according to the social and environmental requirements imposed by a break from the double exploitation of humans and the earth; a break from the sole guiding principle of material accumulation and financial profit, driven by the cult of the commodity and by compulsive consumption, and facilitated by invasive advertising;[21] a break from the enslavement of knowledge to the sole objective of developing new technologies marked by the need for constant innovation and the competitive creation of new consumer needs.

This means that the ecopoietic ecological transition does not only entail a democratically planned economy that is managed at several different levels, according to criteria that are both social and environmental, and that respect both biodiversity and the diversity

[20] The effects of capitalist economic logic and "market fundamentalism" on the environment, and in particular the climate, are well described by Naomi Klein in her best-selling essay (2015a), but she does not draw out the inevitable consequences for a necessary break with a destructive capitalist system and for the institution of a new form of socialism. On the domination over "nature" imposed by capitalism, see in particular Kovel, 2007: 51-94.

[21] See, for example, the proposals formulated by Löwy, 2020: 113-119 and 165-177; see also Kovel & Löwy, 2001, in an "ecosocialist manifesto", and Kovel, 2007: 265-279. It should be noted that the ecopoietic and ecosocialist imperative goes far beyond the social ecology and "communalist" project imagined in the Anglo-American context, in the libertarian movement, which aims at a new municipal rationality and a new ecological humanism: see Bookchin, 2006: 70-71 and 97-110, with particular reference to Aristotle.

of human cultures. As an anthropopoietic transition, it also requires a new conception of of the human. It requires another anthropology than the one that pervades Anglo-American, and now globalised neoliberalism, with its focus on individuals in competition with their peers for the selfish development of their own potential and capacities, exercising an individual and material freedom aimed at personal profit alone, which in reality hinders and limits the freedom of the majority of other human beings. It requires an anthropology based on the principles of proximity and solidarity, in an anthropopoietic and ecopoietic sense…

3. From Exchange Value to Use Value

The concept of the technical arts, whose invention Aeschylus attributes to Prometheus, as useful practices (*ophelémata*) for the civilisation of humans, therefore invites us to return, in a context of capitalist modernity, to one of the founding principles of Marxist economic analysis, namely the distinction between exchange value and use value.

It is worth recalling that this distinction has its origin in an often forgotten passage of Aristotle's *Politics*.[22] Using the example of a shoe, which can be either worn or exchanged, Aristotle draws a distinction between two arts of acquisition (*tékhne ktetiké*): the technical art that underpins the domestic economy, and that which corresponds to an art of accumulating possessions (*khrematistiké*). The former, which relates in particular to agricultural management, involves "the production and storage of the goods necessary and useful for the community life of a city or a family";[23] such a practice of acquisition, which is intended to provide for a "good life" (*agathè zoè*), is limited in its scope. On the contrary, the art of acquisition aimed at the accumulation of goods is unbounded; it is driven by the sole desire to live, and "as such a desire is limitless, one desires an unlimited

---

[22] Aristotle, *Politics* 9, 1256b 40-1258a 19.

[23] 1256b 28-30; see the commentary by Cozzo, 2021: 98-105, with the numerous bibliographical details given in note 15.

number of products to satisfy it".[24] Thus, while exchange may be indispensable insofar as humans, "by nature" (*katà phúsin!*), do not all possess what is necessary, when it is extended to the scale of communities it should be maintained within the limits of a "natural" (*katà phúsin*, once again) autarky; according to this principle, useful things are exchanged for other useful things, and nothing more. The possible combination of that which resembles use value and that which corresponds to exchange value is thus subject to the Promethean criterion of social utility, or civilising utility; and this utilitarian criterion is intended to respond to the needs created by certain deficiencies inherent in the human condition.

Thus, in the first chapter of the first section of the first book of *Capital*, Karl Marx bases his economic reflection on the production of commodities.[25] He defines exchange value as a quantitative relationship that, by means of money, makes the respective use values of the different products of human labour interchangeable. While representing the labour time socially necessary for their production, commodities correspond fundamentally, from the point of view of their use, to a means of subsistence. It is obviously the substitution of exchange value for use value and the exploitation of the labour necessary for the production of commodities that makes capitalist accumulation possible. In short, this development corresponds to Aristotle's account of the desire for unlimited hoarding. Let us recall that, while the material and social conditions of the fourth century incited Aristotle to formulate an opposition between the exchange of goods on the basis of social utility and their appropriation and unlimited accumulation by a minority, he lived in a society in which the majority of productive work was performed by slaves. It was probably this fact, combined with the absence of industrial technological production, that prevented him from developing a theory of the double art of acquisition in terms of the tensions between labour and capital!

---

[24] 1258a 1-3.

[25] Marx, 1976: 125-131.

Nevertheless, Marx's economic theory is dependent on an objectification of nature common to all Western thought in the nineteenth century. Human domination over the forces of nature and the development of humans' own productive forces are the two major themes that mark his critique of capitalism and the foundations of communism. Marx's confidence that further material progress was still to be expected from the industrial revolution, based on the undeniable technical benefits that industrialisation had already brought, did not prevent him from foreseeing the limits and possible destructive consequences of the development of those "productive forces".

As a result of a certain restrictive interpretation of what "material activity" is, one of the foundations of Marxist thought has been transformed into a dogma: "The production of ideas, of conceptions, of consciousness, is at first directly interwoven with the material activity and the material intercourse of men – the language of real life".[26] It is therefore infrastructures that determine superstructures. And at the other end of the causal chain based on human labour, the development of productive forces has as its corollary the domination of nature. This is particularly the case in capitalist agriculture, where all progress "is a progress in the art, not only of robbing the worker, but of robbing the soil [...]. Capitalist production, therefore, only develops the techniques and the degree of combination of the social process of production by simultaneously undermining the original sources of all wealth – the soil and the worker".[27] Thus, particularly in the field of agriculture, capitalist accumulation, with the substitution of exchange value for use value, and the imperative to of constantly increase the former, ends up exhausting and destroying both the workers and their milieu.[28] But Marx did not foresee what

---

[26] Marx & Engels, 1998: 42.

[27] Marx, 1976: 638.

[28] Marx, 1876: I part 7, chap. 24 and I part 4, chap. 15, for citations. These texts have been intelligently commented on by Corcuff, 2012: 99-120; see also Löwy, 2020: 69-80, Saito, 2023: 13-42, as well as, from an eco-feminist perspective, Salleh, 2017: part II § 5. The social and ecological crisis of neoliberal capitalism invites us to revisit the notion of "value": see the proposals made on this subject by Harribey, 2020: 91-142. From a perspective of economic anthropology, relating to gifts-countergifts and accumulation, see Godelier, 2010: 75-99.

would eventually happen under real socialism…

In fact, in order to increase and maximise profits, the exploitation of natural resources is coupled with the exploitation of what are considered, significantly, as mere "human resources". Through relentless extractivism and productive activities that depend almost exclusively on the consumption of hydrocarbons, globalised productivist capitalism has implicitly succeeded in breaking down the artificial barriers between humans and their environment, between culture and nature, but only to destroy both. However, as early as the final report to the Club of Rome in 1972, it became clear that the pollution and other harms inflicted on the environment were due not to demographic growth, but above all to economic growth based on profit, coupled with and accentuated by neo-colonial globalisation, particularly concerning material production. The wave of privatisations that resulted from the spread of neoliberal ideology, first in the Anglo-American sphere from the early 1980s onwards, only accelerated that movement.[29]

We now know the harmful impact on the climate and on human health in particular of unbridled production and the consumption of non-renewable fossil fuels; anarchic production and compulsive consumption centred on the exploitation of coal, hydrocarbons, bituminous sands, or shale gas, in a pure logic of financial profit and capitalist accumulation. We know that, even in the case of digital information and communication technologies, the operation of servers and data centres consumes more than 2% of the world's energy (generally of fossil origin), not to mention the consumption of the computers themselves, the enormous energy cost of streaming, and the polluting waste resulting from devices that are deliberately made to become obsolete after a short period of use.

Consequently, an ecosocialist commitment to social and ecological equity on an anthropopoietic and ecopoietic basis calls for a series of

---

[29] The different stages of this dual movement combining neocolonialism and neoliberalism have recently been clearly traced by Stanziani, 2021: 211-235 and 239-273.

breaks with previous practices:

- a break with the capitalist market economy based on the principles of "free and undistorted" competition and competitiveness, which, as we have seen, leads to the prevalence of exchange value over use value;

- a break with the imperative for unlimited growth measured in particular in quantitative terms of GDP according to the criteria of added value in the goods and services produced;

- a break with a productivism centred on financial profit and involving extractivism, energy waste, various forms of environmental and biosphere pollution, slave-like working conditions, and consumer addiction;

- a break with a globalisation that is subject, through free trade treaties, to the rules of the market and capitalist profit, as well as to the domination of multinationals;

- a break with the neocolonial economic and political domination of rich countries over poorer populations and their environments;

- a break with the ideology of (neo-)liberalism based on individual development and on the generalised commodification not only of human relations, leading in particular to new forms of exclusion and racism, but also of human milieux, which has already caused so much environmental destruction.[30]

4. The Relationship between Humans and their Milieu: Ecopoietic Anthropopoiesis

The fact remains that the material production of goods has been and still is indispensable for the physiological survival, as well as for the anthropopoietic and ecopoietic construction of human communities. It is therefore now necessary to think about the economic practices of humans in relation to their living milieu, as well as the knowledge that guides them, not in terms of "degrowth", but in terms of another

---

[30] For a presentation of the concrete actions that these different breaks require, I refer to my 2020 study; see the references.

kind of growth, an "alter-growth" or, better still, another kind of development. While growth is absolutely necessary in all the countries that have been impoverished by the economic and financial hegemony of the richest nations in relations of neocolonial domination, it must not be based solely on the criterion of increasing GDP.[31] In contrast, a new definition of work should be established which extend beyond the production of goods to include services, including personal care, in ways that would ensure full employment under conditions of social and global justice and environmental protection. On the other hand, economic production itself should undergo an industrial reconversion and be subjected to forms of decentralised planning, through the socialisation of large-scale private property – with relations to the environment redefined according to ecological and social criteria.

Indeed, the material and economic development of communities of women and men must obey human and social criteria that need to be redefined. These could be inspired in particular by Article 25, § 1 of the Universal Declaration of Human Rights:

> *Everyone has the right to a standard of living adequate for the health and well-being of himself and of his family, including food, clothing, housing and medical care and necessary social services, and the right to security in the event of unemployment, sickness, disability, widowhood, old age or other lack of livelihood in circumstances beyond his control.*

In addition to the means of subsistence and, in short, the Promethean technical arts that enable people to adapt empirically to the hazards of mortal life and enjoy decent living conditions, we could add that there should be a right to the necessary democratic access to knowledge, particularly in terms of both health and education.

This is specified, for example, by the "Human Development Index"

---

[31] For a positive critique of the concept of degrowth, see in particular Lavignotte, 2009: 53-80, although a new movement centred around the concept of degrowth has more recently been proposed, with different modalities, by Parrique, 2022: 219-240, who proposes an "economy of post-growth". On the perspectives open by Marx' "degrowth communism", see Saito, 2023: 13-42.

(HDI) created by the UNDP (United Nations Development Programme): this complex index combines measures of a decent standard of living (relative to the gross national income) and life expectancy with measures of knowledge acquisition (calculated using the average length of schooling). From one survey to the next, more specific criteria are added relating to inequalities, for example, in wealth or gender. However the calculations are made, the degree of social integration and access to knowledge are considered essential. Thus, in Article 22 of the UDHR on "social security", the human being is no longer referred to as a person or an individual but, exceptionally, as a "member of society". As such, humans are defined not only by their economic and social rights, but also by their cultural rights, which are "indispensable for [their] dignity and the development of [their] personality".[32]

In such a genuinely anthropopoietic perspective, techniques and technologies, which undoubtedly contribute to ensuring the material basis of human social and cultural emancipation, must be reorientated and reframed, in their inventions and in their uses; and furthermore, this must be done on the base of an anthropopoietic and ecopoietic conception of the basic needs of humans in interaction with their environment. Clearly, only the satisfaction of these immediate material needs concerning food, housing, health, education, and communication can ensure, in a way that grants dignity and peaceful autonomy to each and every person, a social and cultural construction of humans in complex communities, in relation to the living milieux that they inevitably modify, but without degrading or destroying them.

These are therefore the minimum conditions for the anthropopoietic and ecopoietic development of emancipated individuals in social and cultural communities that are themselves emancipated and integrated in their milieux. Any economic deployment, any technological advance should only be subject to social requirements and environmental criteria that take into account the innumerable

---

[32] For an anthropological perspective on this conception of the individual, see Calame, 2012: 15-22.

interactions between people and their living milieux. Under a new system of democratic and political control, both the growth of technical knowledge and the development of "productive forces" should be strictly submitted to democratically elected institutions as well as to the bodies of civil society.

The contemporary paradigm of anthropopoietic ecopoiesis thus requires that the technological be submitted to the ecological and the democratic, and that the economic be submitted to the political, in the broad Greek sense of the term, in a system of supranational coordination that is removed from the economic and financial logics of capital. Rather than an "ethic of degrowth",[33] we should work towards a civic politics of ecosocial progress, in an altermondialist perspective, which necessarily breaks with the neoconservative economic paradigm imposed by neoliberal, oligarchic, patriarchal, and capitalist domination of the planet. Without question, the time has come for a "global ecosocial contract". Such a contract would involve a major departure from the regime of neocolonial domination of the richest countries over the countries of the "Global South" that possess considerable labour power and "natural" resources, and would go far beyond a mere environmentalist policy, which has now been espoused by a form of socialism in thrall to neoliberalism.[34]

Thus, the practical and critical thinking of the *sophoí*, the sages of Classical Greece, invites us to abandon a structural dualism of nature and culture, which their successors contributed to canonising, if only through the creation of distinctions between soul and body, interiority and exteriority, subject and object. Nevertheless, the problem of moral, social, and political responsibility for the fundamental interactions between human beings and an

---

[33] According to the arguments formulated by Lavignotte, 2009: 107-121, following his critique of the desirability of degrowth; see also, Parrique, 2022: 241-268. See also, Kaito, 2023: 171-187.

[34] I am referring here to one of the proposals for an altermondialist transformation put forward by Massiah, 2011: 277-288. Flipo, 2014: 85-94, gives a brief history of green politics; arguably the foundations of such a politics should be anthropological rather than vaguely philosophical. For a critique of the promises made in the name of "Green New Deal", in its various incarnations, see Tanuro, 2020: 303-307.

environment of which they are an integral part still remains to be resolved: we are part of a human-terrestrial ecosystem that is as fragile as it is complex. The survival of humans depends on this milieu and, conversely, the survival of this milieu now depends on human beings in their communities. Moreover, we must not delude ourselves: the concepts of plasticity, permeability, and flexibility that seem to underpin the epistemology of the life sciences are themselves products of the neoliberal paradigm... The fact remains that these concepts currently provide us with the terms in which to think, in the here and now, about the reciprocal and complex actions between, on the one hand, the individuals and communities that contribute to their own social construction and, on the other hand, the terrestrial, animal, and climatic milieux on which they depend: men and women shape and modify those milieux in accordance with their forms of life, their lifestyles, their technical and social practices, and their cultural representations.

On the condition that it is used in a decentred manner and viewed as a culture of difference, Greek knowledge makes it possible to avoid the misunderstandings fostered by the reification of nature. In our critical detour via the ancient world, the sages of Classical Greece invite us to rethink not only the anthropological conception that has enshrined the opposition between nature and culture, but also the neoliberal paradigm that has implicitly adopted it in order to legitimise its destructive depredations on our human and environmental milieu. In this perspective, contemporary liberal economists insist on attributing an "intrinsic economic value" to a reified nature.[35] Whether we attempt to commodify the environment of human communities by reifying it into a nature subject to exchange value (under the pretext of a use value) or whether, on the contrary, we claim to attribute rights to this milieu by giving it an anthropomorphic identity as Nature (if not Mother Earth), or even by enclosing it in the concept of an "Earth System", it is always the

---

[35] See Harribey, 2013: 158-205, for a detailed critique of attempts to estimate the value of nature, a concept which he calls a "perfect oxymoron" ; see also 206-211, on nature as a subject of rights (!), and Calame, 2020-21.

complex interactions between humans in communities and their different material, social, and cultural milieux that are ignored. A critical altermondialist ecosocialism must, on the contrary, integrate these interactions between humans and their environment in an attempt to master them while developing them in a constructive way, according to ecosocial criteria.

We can therefore conclude by drawing on the words of the wise physiologist Democritus: "Nature [*phúsis*] and education [*didakhê*] are comparable. Indeed, education shapes the rhythm [*metarusmoî*] of man and in so doing creates nature [*phusiopoieî*]".[36] What better expression could there be of the dynamic collaboration of what we call the innate and the acquired, the anthropopoietic and ecopoietic making of the human, in interaction with *phúsis* – a *phúsis*, we should add, that also includes the living milieu and which implies a certain rhythm on the part of the human, if only in the pedagogical relationship. In short, in the Greek sense, nature is culture.

[36] Democritus, fr. 68 B 33 Diels-Kranz (= 27. Atom. D403 Laks-Most); cf. fr. 278 (= 27. Atom. D395 Laks-Most).

Bibliography

AFFERGAN F., BORUTTI S., CALAME C., FABIETTI U., KILANI M., REMOTTI F., *Figures de l'humain. Les représentations de l'anthropologie*, Paris, Éditions de l'EHESS, 2003

d'ALEMBERT J. LE ROND, "Nature", *Encyclopédie ou Dictionnaire raisonné des arts, des sciences et des métiers par une société des gens de lettres*, Neuchâtel, Samuel Faulche, 1765, pp. 40-41

ATTAC, *Les OGM en guerre contre la société*, Paris, Mille et une nuits, 2005

—, *La Nature n'a pas de prix. Les méprises de l'économie verte*, Paris, Les Liens qui Libèrent, 2012

AZAM G., *Osons rester humain. Les impasses de la toute-puissance*, Paris, Les Liens qui Libèrent, 2015

BALDRY H. C., *The Unity of Mankind in Greek Thought*, Cambridge, Cambridge University Press, 1965

BENVENISTE E., *Noms d'agent et noms d'action en indo-européen*, Paris, A. Maisonneuve, 1975 (original edition: 1948)

BERQUE A., *Écoumène. Introduction à l'étude des milieux humains*, Paris, Belin, 2010 (2nd ed.)

—, *Poétique de la Terre. Histoire naturelle et histoire humaine, essais de mésologie,* Paris, Belin, 2014. English translation: *Poetics of the Earth. Natural History and Human History*, trans. A.-M. Feenberb-Dibon, Abingdon, Routledge, 1999

—, "L'embrayage nature/culture. Des intuitions watsujiennes à une mésologie de l'évolution", à paraître

BIHR A., *La Novlangue néolibérale. La rhétorique du fétichisme capitaliste*, Lausanne, Éditions page deux, 2007

BONNEUIL Ch., FRESSOZ J.-B., *L'Événement anthropocène. La Terre, l'histoire et nous*, Paris, Seuil, 2016 (2nd ed.)

BOOKCHIN M., *Social Ecology and Communalism*, Oakland CA, AK Press, 2006

BORUTTI S., *Filosofia dei sensi. Estetica del pensiero tra filosofia, arte e letteratura*, Rome, Cortina, 2006

BOUAMAMA S., "Mondialisation capitaliste, eurocentrisme et immigration. Une prolétarisation du monde", in C. Calame, A. Fabart (eds.), 2020, pp. 117-140

BOYER-BÉVIÈRE B., MOINE-DUPUIS I. (eds.), *L'humain en transformation. Entre transhumanisme et humanité,* special issue, *Cahiers Droits, Sciences & Technologies*, 11, 2020, https://journals.openedition.org/cdst/2252

BUCCHERI, A., "Costruire l'umano in termini vegetali. *Phúo* e *phúsis* nella tragedia greca", *I Quaderni del Ramo d'Oro on-line* 5, 2012, pp. 137-163, http://www.qro.unisi.it/frontend/node/138

BUFFON G.-L. Leclerc Comte de, *Œuvres complètes IV. Histoire naturelle de l'Homme,* Paris, Imprimerie Royale, 1774

—, *Penser les hommes à travers les plantes: métaphores botaniques du corps et de la parenté dans la poésie grecque archaïque et classique*, Grenoble, Jérôme Millon (to be published)

—, *Les Époques de la nature*, 2 vol., Paris, Imprimerie Royale, 1780

BURGART GOUTAL J., *Être écoféministe. Théories et pratiques,* Paris, L'échappée, 2020

CALAME C., "Les figures grecques du gigantesque", *Communications* 42, 1985, pp. 147-171, reprinted in *Sentiers transversaux. Entre poétiques grecques et politiques contemporaines*, Grenoble, Jérôme Millon, 2008, pp. 109-132

—, "Nature humaine et environnement: Le racisme bien tempéré d'Hippocrate", in *Sciences et racisme*, Lausanne, Payot, 1986, pp. 77-99, reprinted in *Masques d'autorité. Fiction et pragmatique dans la poétique grecque antique*, Paris, Les Belles Lettres, 2005, pp. 237-273

—, "Interprétation et traduction des cultures. Les catégories de la pensée et du discours anthropologique", *L'Homme* 163, 2002, pp. 51-78

—, *Pratiques poétiques de la mémoire. Représentations de l'espace-temps en Grèce ancienne*, Paris, La Découverte, 2006

CALAME C. (ed.), *Identités de l'individu contemporain*, Paris, Textuel, 2008

—, Prométhée généticien. Profits techniques et usages de métaphores, Paris, Les Belles

Lettres, 2010

—, "The Pragmatics of "Myth" in Plato's Dialogues: The Story of Prometheus in the *Protagoras*", in C. Collobert, P. Destrée, F. J. Gonzalez (eds.), *Plato and Myth. Studies in the Use and Status of Platonic Myths*, Leiden, Boston, Brill, 2012, pp. 127-143

—, "Pour une transition écosocialiste en rupture avec le capitalisme. Arguments et propositions", *Les Possibles* 25, 2020, pp. 1-8, https://france.attac.org/nos-publications/les-possibles/numero-25-automne-2020/debats/article/pour-une-transition-ecosocialiste-en-rupture-avec-le-capitalisme-   arguments-et

—, "L'homme en société et ses relations avec l'environnement. Ni nature, ni Gaïa", *Les Possibles* 26, 2020-21, pp. 1-11, https://france.attac.org/nos-publications/les-possibles/numero-26-hiver-2020-2021/dossier-vers-la-fin-de-la-separation-societe-nature/article/l-homme-en-societe-et-ses-relations-techniques-avec-l-environnement-ni-nature

CALAME C., FABART A., (eds.), *Migrations forcées, discriminations et exclusions. Les enjeux de politiques néocoloniales*, Vulaines-sur-Seine, Éditions du Croquant, 2020

CALAME C., FABART A., "Causes et effets des migrations contraintes. Propositions altermondialistes", in C. Calame, A. Fabart (eds.), 2020, pp. 163-186

CALAME C., KILANI M. (eds.), *La Fabrication de l'humain dans les cultures et en anthropologie*, Lausanne, Payot, 1999

CANGUILHEM G., *Knowledge of Life*, trans. S. Geroulanos, D. Ginsburg, New York, Fordham University Press, 2008 (original edition: 1952)

CERRI G., *Il linguaggio politico nel Prometeo di Eschilo. Saggio di semantica*, Rome, Ateneo, 1975

CORCUFF Ph., *Marx XXIᵉ siècle. Textes commentés*, Paris, Textuel, 2012

COZZO A., "Dimensioni umane della questione ecologica nella Grecia antica", in C. Calame, *L'uomo e il suo ambiente. Al di là dell'opposizione natura/cultura*, Palermo, Sellerio, 2021, pp. 87-112

CUCHE D., La Notion de culture dans les sciences sociales, Paris, La Découverte, 1996

DESCARTES R., *Discourse on Method and Meditations on First Philosophy*, trans. D Cress, Indianapolis, IN, Hackett, 1998 (original edition: Leiden, Jan Maire, 1637)

DESCOLA Ph., "Constructing Nature. Symbolic Ecology and Social Practice", in Ph. Descola, G. Pálsson (eds.), *Nature and Society. Anthropological Perspectives*, London & New York, Routledge, 1996, pp. 83-102

—, *Par-delà nature et culture*, Paris, Gallimard, 2005

—, Diversité des natures, diversité des cultures, Paris, Bayard, 2010

DIANTEILL E., "Anthropologie culturelle ou anthropologie sociale? Une dispute transatlantique", *Année sociologique* 62, 2012, pp. 93-122

DUCHET M., *Anthropologie et histoire au siècle des Lumières*, Paris, Albin Michel, 1995 (original edition: Paris, La Découverte, 1971)

DURKHEIM E., MAUSS M., "Note on the Concept of Civilisation", in M. Mauss, *Techniques, Technology and Civilisation*, ed. Nathan Schlanger, New York, Durkheim Press/Berghahn Books, 2009, pp. 35-40 (original edition: *Année sociologique* 12, 1913)

FLIPO F., Pour une philosophie politique écologiste, Paris, Textuel, 2014

GALISSOT R., KILANI M., RIVERA A., *L'Imbroglio ethnique. En quatorze mots clés*, Lausanne, Payot, 2000

GEERTZ C., *The Interpretation of Cultures. Selected Essays*, New York, Basic Books, 1973

GIORGIANNI F., "Uomini e technai nell'ambiente. Tra *Arie, acque, luoghi e Prometeo incantenato*", in C. Calame, *L'uomo e il suo ambiente. Al di là dell'opposizione natura/cultura*, Palermo, Sellerio, 2021, pp. 113-137

GODELIER M., *Au fondement des sociétés humaines. Ce que nous apprend l'anthropologie*, Paris, Flammarion, 2010 (2ⁿᵈ ed.)

GUESPIN-MICHEL J., *Émancipation et pensée du complexe*, Paris, Éditions du Croquant, 2015

GUTHRIE W. K. C., *The Sophists*, Cambridge, Cambridge University Press, 1971

HARRIBEY J.-M., *La Richesse, la valeur et l'inestimable. Fondements d'une critique socio-écologique de l'économie capitaliste*, Paris, Les Liens qui Libèrent, 2013

HEINIMANN F., *Nomos und Phusis. Herkunft und Bedeutung einer Antithese im Griechischen Denken des 5. Jahrhunderts*, Basel, Reinhardt, 1954

HERDER J. G., *Ideen zur Philosophie der Geschichte der Menschheit*, Frankfurt a/M., Deutscher Klassiker Verlag, 1989 (original edition: Riga & Leipzig, J. F. Hartknoch, 1784-1791). French translation: *Idées pour la philosophie de l'histoire de l'humanité*, Paris, F. G. Levrault, 1834

HERITIER F., *Masculin/féminin. La pensée de la différence*, Paris, Odile Jacob, 1996

HOMER, *The Iliad*, trans. A. T. Murray, Cambridge, MA, Harvard University Press, 1924

KEMPF H., *Pour sauver la planète, sortez du capitalisme*, Paris, Seuil, 2009

KILANI M., *Anthropologie. Du local au global*, Paris, Armand Colin, 2009

KLEIN N., *Tout peut changer. Capitalisme et changement climatique*, Paris, Actes Sud/Lux, 2015a

KLEIN N. et al., *Crime climatique stop! L'appel de la société civile*, Paris, Seuil, 2015b

KOVEL J., *The Enemy of Nature. The End of Capitalism or the End of the World?* London, Zed books, 2007 (2nd ed.)

KOVEL J., LÖWY M., "An Ecosocialist Manifesto", Paris, 2001, http://environment-ecology.com/political-ecology/436-an-ecosocialist-manifesto.html

LATOUR B., *Face à Gaïa. Huit conférences sur le Nouveau Régime Climatique*, Paris, La Découverte, 2015a

LATOUR B., "Telling Friends from Foes in the Time of the Anthropocene", in C. Hamilton, Ch. Bonneuil, F. Gemenne (eds.), *The Anthropocene and the Global Environmental Crisis. Rethinking Modernity in a New Epoch*, Oxford & New York, Routledge, 2015b, pp. 145-155

LATOUR B., *Où atterrir? Comment s'orienter en politique*, Paris, La Découverte, 2017

LATOUR B., SCHULTZ N., *Mémo sur la nouvelle classe écologique*, Paris, La Découverte, 2022

LAVIGNOTTE S., *La Décroissance est-elle souhaitable?* Paris, Textuel, 2009

LESTEL D., *Les Origines animales de la culture*, Paris, Flammarion, 2003 (2nd ed.)

LÉVI-STRAUSS C., *Les Structures élémentaires de la parenté*, Paris & La Haye, Mouton, 1967 (original edition: Paris, Plon, 1947)

—, *The Elementary Structures of Kinship*, trans. J. Bell, J. Sturmer, R. Needham, Boston, MA, Beacon Press, 1969 (original edition: Paris, Plon, 1947)

—, *Structural Anthropology: Volume 2*, trans. M. Layton, Harmondsworth, Penguin, 1978 (original edition: Paris, Plon, 1973)

LEWIS S. L, MASLIN M. A., "Defining the Anthropocene", *Nature* 519, 2015, pp. 171-80

LLOYD G. E. R., *Methods and Problems in Greek Sciences*, Cambridge, Cambridge University Press, 1991

—, *Being, Humanity and Understanding. Studies in Ancient and Modern Societies*, Oxford, Oxford University Press, 2012

LONGO O., "L'antropologia", in Cambiano G., Canfora L., Lanza D. (eds.), *Lo spazio letterario della Grecia antica* II. *La ricezione e l'attualizzazione del testo*, Rome, Salerno, 1995, pp. 737-762

—, "La mano dell'uomo da Aristotele a Galeno", *Quaderni Urbinati di Cultura Classica* 95, 2000, pp. 7-29

LÖWY M., *Qu'est-ce que l'écosocialisme?*, Montreuil, Le Temps des Cerises, 2020 (2nd ed.)

MACÉ A, "La naissance de la nature en Grèce ancienne", in S. Haber, A. Macé (eds.), *Anciens et Modernes par-delà nature et société*, Besançon, Presses universitaires de Franche-Comté, 2012, pp. 47-84

MALINOWSKI B., *A Scientific Theory of Culture*, New York, Galaxy Books, 1961

MARX K., *Capital. A Critique of Political Economy: Volume One*, trans. B. Fowkes, London, Penguin, 1976 (original edition: Hamburg, Otto Meissner, 1867)

MARX K., ENGELS F., *The German Ideology*, New York, Prometheus Books, 1998 (original edition: Berlin, Friedrich Engels Verlag, 1932)

MASSIAH G., *Une Stratégie altermondialiste*, Paris, La Découverte, 2011

MERCHANT C., *The Death of Nature. Women, Ecology and the Scientific Revolution*, San Francisco,

Harper & Row,1980 (3d ed: 2020)

MILLET D., TOUSSAINT E., *La Crise, quelles crises?* Bruxelles, Éditions Aden – CADTM, 2010

MORGAN K. A., *Myth and Philosophy: From the Presocratics to Plato*, Cambridge, Cambridge University Press, 2000

PARRIQUE T., *Ralentir ou périr. L'économie de la décroissance*, Paris, Seuil, 2022

PUCCI P., *The Songs of the Sirens. Essays on Homer*, Lanham, Boulder, New York, & Oxford, Rowman & Littlefield, 1998

REMOTTI F., "Thèses pour une perspective anthropopoiétique", in C. Calame, M. Kilani (eds.), 1999, pp. 15-31

—, *Fare umanità. I drammi dell'antropo-poiesi*, Rome & Bari, Laterza, 2013

RIVERA A., "La construction de la nature et de la culture dans la relation homme-animal", in C. Calame, M. Kilani (eds.), 1999, pp. 49-72

ROSE S., KAMIN L. J., LEWONTIN R. C., *Not in Our Genes. Biology, Ideology, and Human Nature*, Hardmondsworth, Pelican Books, 1984

ROSE H., ROSE S., *Genes, Cells and Brains. The Promethean Promises of the New Biology*, London & New York, Verso, 2012

ROUSSEAU J.-J., *Discourse on the Origin of Inequality*, trans. D. Cress, Indianapolis, IN, Hackett, 1992 (original edition: Amsterdam, Marc Michel Rey, 1755)

SAHLINS M., *The Western Illusion of Human Nature. With Reflections on the Long History of Hierarchy, Equality, and the Sublimation of Anarchy in the West, and Comparative Notes on Other Conceptions of the Human Condition*, Chicago, Prickly Paradigm Press, 2008

SAITO K., *Marx in the Anthropocene. Towards the Idea of Degrowth Communism*, Cambridge, Cambridge University Press, 2023

SAÏD S., *Sophiste et tyran ou le problème du* Prométhée enchaîné, Paris, Klincksieck, 1975

SALLEH A., *Ecofeminism as Politics. Nature, Marx and the Postmodern*, New York, Zed Books, 2017 (2nd ed.)

SCHAEFFER J.-M., *La Fin de l'exception humaine*, Paris, Gallimard, 2007

SHIVA V., *Staying Alive. Ecology and Development*, New Dehli & London, Kali for Women – Zed Books, 1988

SINAÏ A., "Le destin des sociétés industrielles", in A. Sinaï (ed.), *Penser la décroissance. Politiques de l'anthropocène*, Paris, Presses de Sciences Po, 2013, pp. 23-48

SOLÓN P., "Droits de la Terre-Mère. Vers une communauté de la Terre", in ATTAC, *Le monde qui émerge. Les alternatives qui peuvent tout changer*, Paris, Les Liens qui libèrent, 2017, pp. 21-61

SPRETNAK Ch., *Lost Goddesses of Early Greece. A Collection of Pre-Hellenic Myths*, Boston, Beacon Press, 1992 (3rd ed.; original edition: 1978)

STANZIANI A., *Capital Terre. Une histoire longue du monde d'après (XIIᵉ-XXIᵉ siècle)*, Paris, Payot, 2021

TANURO D., *Trop tard pour être pessimiste! Écosocialisme ou effondrement*, Paris, Textuel, 2020

TESTART J., SINAÏ A., BOURGAIN C., *Labo Planète ou Comment 2030 se prépare sans les citoyens*, Paris, Mille et une Nuits, 2010.

THOMAS R., *Herodotus in Context. Ethnography, Science and the Art of Persuasion*, Cambridge, Cambridge University Press, 2000

TRÉPANIER S., *Empedocles. An Interpretation*, New York & London, Routledge, 2004

TYLOR E. B., *Primitive Culture. Researches in the Development of Mythology, Philosophy, Religion, Art and Custom*, 2 vol., London, Murray, 1871

VEGETTI M., *Il coltello e lo stile*, Milano, Mondadori, 1987 (2nd ed.)

VERNANT J.-P., "Prométhée et la fonction technique", in *Mythe et pensée chez les Grecs. Études de psychologie historique*, Paris, Maspero, 1966 (original edition: *Journal de psychologie normale et pathologique* 45, 1952, pp. 419-429)

—, "À la table des hommes. Mythe de fondation du sacrifice chez Hésiode", in Detienne M. et Vernant J.-P., *La Cuisine du sacrifice en pays grec*, Paris, Gallimard, 1979, pp. 37-132

VIDAL-NAQUET P., "Valeurs religieuses et mythiques de la terre et du sacrifice dans l'*Odyssée*", *Annales E. S. C.* 25, 1970, pp. 1278-1297, reprinted in *Le Chasseur noir. Formes de pensée et formes de société dans le monde grec*, Paris, La Découverte, 1983 (2nd ed.), pp. 39-68

VON UEXKÜLL J., *Umwelt und Innenwelt der Tiere*, Berlin, J. Springer, 1921 (2nd ed.)

WARIN I., "La notion de *technè* en Grèce ancienne", *Artefact* 15, 2021, pp. 43-60

WITTGENSTEIN L., *Tractatus Logico-Philosophicus. Centenary Edition*, ed. Luciano Bazzocchi, trans. B. McGuinness, D. Pears, London, Anthem Press, 2021 (original edition: London, Kegan Paul, Trench, Trubner & Co., 1922)

www.ingramcontent.com/pod-product-compliance
Lightning Source LLC
Chambersburg PA
CBHW050655270326
41927CB00012B/3046